Today's Hope

A DAILY DEVOTIONAL

GEOFFREY GORDON

REASON
WITH ROBDON

Scripture references are taken from the King James Version of the Bible. The emphasis in Scripture quotations is added by the Author.

You may contact the author at 1-876-258-1108.

First edition

ISBN: 978-1-990266-11-9

Contents

Preface

This book is a result of several years of sharing my morning devotions with my many friends and family at home and abroad.

My motivation has been the inspiration of the Holy Ghost. The devotions are therefore designed to uplift, warn, encourage, teach, and admonish.

As a Bible teacher, I have also been blessed with the resources to provide historical and biblical data to share in these devotions.

I have faced many challenges as well as encouragement throughout this journey. There were times when I had to sit up late at nights to compile my devotions for the following day. There were also times when there did not seem to be enough hours in the day to complete my tasks.

My writings span a period of ten years and by the grace of God, they have now transitioned into a book. May souls be blessed, strengthened, renewed, sinners turn to Christ and darkness be made light as you read this book.

Acknowledgement

To the Person of the Holy Spirit, my Comforter and Friend who has energised and enabled me to accomplish this task - my efforts would have been futile had He not been there to motive and encourage me when the mission seemed overwhelming and daunting.

Once this devotional started to go from a concept in my head to a manuscript, there were many persons involved who deserve to be acknowledged. The task of completing this book could not be possible without these individuals' collaborative and supportive efforts. First, I would like to acknowledge my manager Mr Steve Sortie. Thank you for your suggestions, advice, and friendship. You have faithfully managed and organized this project so competently.

Thanks to Rev Dr Leticia McPherson, the editor and publishing manager. We are indebted to you for your expertise. Thanks to everyone on the publishing team.

To my family members and friends, thanks for the support received through encouragement, motivation, and prayer. Thanks to Anna-Kaye Mighty, my niece who is responsible for the photograph. To Delano Mighty, my nephew and his wife Amanda, thank you for your beautiful cover illustration. Your creativity has been truly inspiring.

Finally, to all those who have been a part of my getting there:

Rev. Denzil Jack, Rev. Al Miller, Bishop Orville Moore, Rev Marcus Williams, Pastor Felitia Watson, Pastor Walton Wilson, Ms Tracy Ann Myers, Ms Janet Mitchell, Ms Kayan Nash, Ms Elaine Edwards, Ms Mary Bryan, and Mr Craig Butler.

Most of all I want to thank my wife Vivienne for her incredible heart, and as in all things, her invaluable support. She is as important to this book getting done as I am.

All of you have helped to inspire me to make this devotional a success. I will always be grateful to you all for your help and encouragement. May God bless you always.

Introduction

For almost a decade, inspired by God, I have collected my thoughts in a daily devotional. Every morning, I share these reflections with my friends and family. It inspires them to follow Christ with heart, mind, soul, and strength. Now, I am sharing these treasures with you.

Today's Hope is a compilation of devotions written to inspire confidence, engender change and engage hearts with the Word of God. Based on the book of Ezekiel, these devotionals take a deep dive into the Word, connecting real-life situations to the stories outlined in the Bible. This book offers hope and light in a world of chaos and darkness. As you go through this book on your daily sojourn with the Lord, I pray you will radiate God's love and that you will share this word of hope with those around you. Prayerfully reflect with me on the day ahead as we dive in.

I wait for the Lord, my soul doth wait, and in his word do I hope.
- Psalm 130:5

Day 1

"You must speak My words to them whether they listen or fail to listen, for they are rebellious. You, son of man listen to what I say to you. Do not rebel like that rebellious house; open your mouth and eat what I give you."

Eze 2:7-8

Go, I Send You: The Word of the Lord.

The nation of Israel was steep in sin and deeply rebellious. They rebelled against God and His laws. As a result, God called, equipped, and sent Ezekiel to warn them to turn from their lives of sin.

God knew that many would not heed the warning through His prophet. Nonetheless, Ezekiel was still sent. God warned Ezekiel not to disobey His command like those of his countrymen who rebelled against Him. His duty was to warn them, whether they listened to him.

Today, the same message is relevant: 'Go! I send you.' Sin is rampant and many today neither want God nor are they interested in His ordinances. Some want what God gives but to them, God Himself is irrelevant. Many humans have become so materialistic that their possessions have become their gods. The behaviour of many would suggest that Almighty God does not exist. Some are not only sinful, but they encourage others to sin against The One True God. These days, many things that were wrong in the past are now declared to be right. However, something is not declared right simply because the government, legislators, activists, or the majority say so. Once it is sin, it remains sin. If the Lord said it is wrong, it is wrong.

In these closing hours, men have become lovers of themselves. Many who should name the name of Christ have denied the power of God. It must be made known that those who deny the power of God have denied God Himself.

God's uncompromising Word must be preached to the world because many are on their way to a Godless Hell and need to hear about the love of God. God has called us, equipped us and He has sent us with His Word of repentance to tell the nations to repent and turn to Him. The Gospel must be preached by those who have accepted Jesus Christ as Lord and Saviour. It is not only a select few who should go on the byways, streets, and everywhere with the Gospel. We all need to.

If we disobey the Command of God to go and evangelise the world, we might find ourselves in trouble with the Lord. Brothers and sisters, may we never send anyone to Hell because we refuse to minister the Gospel to them. We must obey the Lord, as this is our spiritual and moral responsibility. Let it not be that someone's blood rests upon our head because we did not present the Gospel to him/her.

In St. Matthew 28:16-20, Jesus gave the Great Commission to His disciples, to take the Gospel to all the Earth. Today, we who are His disciples are expected to follow the same directive.

Dearly beloved, let us make every effort to present the Gospel of Jesus Christ to the lost. Our call is to make the presentation of the Gospel, whether people want to listen. May God help us to do our part since it is He who has sent us.

Day 2

The Word of the Lord came to me: "Still son of man, this is what the Sovereign Lord says to the land of Israel: The end! The end has come upon the four corners of the land. The end is now upon you and I will unleash My anger against you. I will judge you according to your conduct and repay you for all your detestable practices. I will not look on you with pity or spare you; I will surely repay you for your conduct and the detestable practices among you. Then you will know that I Am The Lord."

Eze 7:1-4

The End!

Ezekiel was given the task to speak to a rebellious people about their conduct. Israel had divorced Almighty God and prostrated herself to idols. Idolatry was the order of the day, the behaviour of a nation gone to detestable practices. Spiritual adultery was in full swing.

Is this the same situation Jamaica has found herself in? We have more churches per square mile than any other nation. Yet, many of our Churches are becoming less populated. Truth is, many do not want God.

How about many Christians today? Has God become secondary? What about witnessing to the world? Is it that money, family, career, position, or possession has replaced God? Know this for sure: anything or anyone who becomes our priority is our god, our idol.

God clearly declared His disgust concerning Israel. He hated the detestable practices of idolatry. He signalled His intent to exact punishment upon a nation He chose over all others. Let us not fool ourselves into believing that we are so special to God or that we are under a better covenant, so we can do whatever we choose and will not face punishment. Israel was special, but when they committed spiritual adultery, God punished them. Think again!

The end is near. May we be ready to meet God. May we spend time seeking God in prayer, fasting and through the Word. May we be alert and take note that the harvest is ripe, and we need to win lost souls at any cost. The Lord is relying on us. We are His mouthpiece in this generation. We are His ambassadors to the world, and the world needs us. Let us work now while it is still day because the night is fast approaching.

The coming of The Lord is extremely near! Therefore, arise and live for God: men, women, boys, and girls!

Day 3

The Spirit lifted me up between Earth and Heaven and in visions of God, He took me to Jerusalem, to the entrance to the north gate of the inner court, where the idol that provokes to jealousy stood. So I went in and looked, and I saw portrayed all over the walls all kinds of crawling things and detestable animals and all the idols of the House of Israel. In front of them stood seventy elders of the House of Israel, and Jaazaniah son of Shaphan was standing among them. Each had a censer in his hand, and a fragrant cloud of incense was rising. He then brought me into the inner court of the House of the Lord, and there at the entrance of the temple, between the portico and the altar, were about twenty five men. With their backs towards the temple of the Lord and their faces towards the east, they were bowing down to the sun in the east.

Eze 8:3b, 10-11 & 16

Idolatry in the Church

During the days of Ezekiel, idolatry was at its peak. The leaders of Israel, elders of the Temple and regular citizens worshipped false gods. Idolatry was so common that the utter disrespect towards God was on full view for all to see. Yet those practising it believed they were hidden from God.

Almighty God was seemingly expelled from His house, the Temple, by leaders who prostrated themselves to demons. This was utter contempt to God and brought curses upon the people. Ah, beloved, Almighty God was deeply angry with Israel and action from Him was inevitable.

Today, idolatry has earned its way into many church assemblies, and many are worshippers of created things and beings than the Creator.

It is so sad that Mary the mother of Jesus is worshipped in Catholic circles, as more homage is paid to her than God Himself. Some Christians have become worshippers of their pastors, institutions, programmes, gadgets, and denominations - not to mention those who worship their positions in the church or their titles. Friends, the sad reality is that people and possessions for many have taken the place of God. What a travesty and a controversy!

God hates idolatry. It is detestable in His eyes and He clearly warned in Exodus 20:3, "You shall have no other gods before Me." God knew well that the consequence of idolatry was severe punishment, hence His stern warning.

My brothers and sisters in Christ, who is the first place in your life today? Are our Bibles seldom read? What about spending quality time in prayer and fasting with our Maker? Is there a burden on your heart for lost souls? Have we taken time to minister to those *en route* to Hell? Have we spent so much time at our jobs seeking to make money that we have no time for God? Has money become our primary focus? Have our vehicles become our gods, so much so that we cannot assist a fellow Christian with a ride because the car is too 'criss?' May God help us if we are idol worshippers!

Israel led a detestable lifestyle, worshipping idols of different sorts and God was angry. What about us, friends? Have we left the way of the Lord for idols? If so, let us be clear: Almighty God accepts no rivals.

Day 4

Then the glory of the Lord rose from above the cherubim and moved to the threshold of the temple. The cloud filled the temple, and the court was full of the radiance of the glory of the Lord. Then the glory of the Lord departed from over the threshold of the temple and stopped above the cherubim.

Eze 10:4 & 18

The Glory of God Departs

The temple of God in Israel was not only a sanctuary for worship but a symbol of Almighty God's presence. God's presence displayed awesomely whenever His people respected and honoured Him.

God signalled His nearness to His people by presenting Himself in His glorious form, and His marvellous presence filled the temple.

Many Israelites during Ezekiel's time wanted the blessings of God, but they did not want God Himself. They understood the glory of God offered them many blessings, including protection from their enemies. Oh yes, beloved, to some those blessings were enough. However, God will never be subjected to men using Him merely to get by. Consequently, His glory departed from the temple, and with the glory left His protection.

The Lord shared a wonderful and terrible truth with me: some people worship the anointing and those anointed but not the Anointer Himself. So many just want the anointing to do exploits, but truly not The One Who offers the anointing. When one truly desires God and seeks Him, His anointing is present.

So, what or who is it that we want? Do we want the glory of God and His anointing? Or do we want Almighty God Himself?

People are normally attracted to men and women of God who are filled with the anointing and many will worship them. God forbid! God, however, has called us to seek and worship Him and Him Only.

Since we are His children, may we maintain His anointing/glory by sincerely living for Him. May our spirits, souls and bodies be in full submission to Him, and may His Holy Spirit be happy to indwell us. May His glory remain and never depart.

Day 5

Some of the elders of Israel came to me and sat down in front of me. Then the word of the Lord came to me: "Son of man, these men have set up idols in their hearts and put wicked stumbling blocks before their faces. Should I let them enquire of Me at all?"

Eze 13:1-3

A Hapless Israel, God's Glory Already Gone

Generally, Israel did not want God, yet their elders steep in idolatry hypocritically claimed they were seeking Him. Their attitude reflected neglect and aggression to God's ordinances. Those Israelites in Ezekiel's days had a short memory and it seemed they had mental, emotional, spiritual, and physical amnesia. With the great intervention God made in delivering their forebears from Egypt and the mighty miracles they experienced, no other nations had seen the mighty move of God as they did. Yet they turned their backs on the Lord. They hated God and His presence and did not want Him anywhere near them.

Although God warned them of their idolatry and contemptuous disregard towards Him and His ordinances, they did not take heed and God removed His presence and glory from the temple and subsequently from the land of Israel.

In many churches today, the glory of God has already gone. Some congregations are operating on former blessings — a shadow of the past. If a church does not conduct prayer meetings or seldomly does, or if Bible Studies are not seen as important, then that Church has lost its purpose. If the Holy

10

Spirit is not a priority in a congregation, the glory of God has already departed.

Similarly, if our individual lives refuse to reflect God's glory, we are in deep trouble. If the Word of God and the Holy Spirit are not the first place in our lives, we are engaging in idolatry and clearly, the glory of God cannot be reflected through us. It is about sacrificing all for Jesus. Remember, He sacrificed His all for you and me. He expects our all so we can reflect His glory - or otherwise nothing at all. In St. Luke 14:33, He revealed, "In the same way, any of you who does not give up everything he has cannot be My disciple." Only a true disciple of God and a church that places God first can reflect His glory.

If the Lord is not in charge, one is on his or her own, and the glory of God is already gone. When there is no glory in the Church, people will not get saved, healed, delivered, set free and chaos and confusion will take centre stage. Furthermore, the devil will continue to sit in church undisturbed and undetected. What a catastrophe!

Beloved, may our lives be filled with the Holy Spirit continually, with the Word of God completely guiding us. In this way, God's glory will be seen. However, if we reject the Holy Spirit and God's ordinances and are aggressive to His will, placing His Word lower than first in our lives, then let us not fool ourselves to believe that we are on good terms with Him. Be sure that the glory is already gone.

Israel rejected God and His commandments, and the glory of God departed. May we take note of what happened to them and not emulate their behaviour.

Day 6

The Word of the Lord came to me: "Son of man, you are living among a rebellious people. They have eyes to see but do not see and ears to hear but do not hear, for they are a rebellious people."

Eze 12:1-2

Eyes Without Seeing. Ears Without Hearing.

Whilst growing up in my formative years, my mother echoed a statement more than once to me: *"Bwoy, wah mek yu no hear wen piipl taak tu yu? A stik bruk ina yu ears?"* Such an utterance would come when something was commanded of me, but instead, I did the reverse. Thereafter a stern consequence followed for not listening or following parental instructions — usually a spanking.

God told Ezekiel that the people he was sent to had ears but did not hear. This suggests that they refused to listen to the Word from God that was said to them. Their actions were deliberate as they chose to rebel against God, His Word, and His prophet. In the same way, they had eyes but refused to see the very hole they were falling into, even when warned about the pitfalls. Ezekiel's message was one given by God, but the choice was made by the Israelites not to pay him any attention.

While building an ark on instructions from God, people thought Noah was crazy. They did not listen to his message - and even ridiculed him - when he warned them to change their sinful and rebellious lifestyle. They only realised that what he said to them was not crazy when, for the very first time in history, the rains began. Noah's warnings became a reality to them all too late.

Is there any difference today? The Gospel of Jesus Christ is being preached and presented in different forms to people, yet many do not listen. Some behave as if the message is not true and pay scant regard to what is being said. The truth is, as was in the days of Noah, so it will be. Many will hear the Gospel but not pay any attention to it. Too late, too late shall be their cry, and many will say, 'If only I had listened and put into practice what the preacher had said, I would not have been lost.'

In this modern age, many will not listen to the message of the Kingdom of God, while some will hear and destructively criticize what is said. Others still will persecute us because of God's message. However, it is still our duty to present them with the Gospel of Jesus Christ. No amount of opposition, persecution or lack of resources should stop us from presenting the Gospel to the lost. The harvest is ripe and we who are labourers must work efficiently for the Lord to reap the harvest.

Oh, what sadness to those who have eyes to see but not seeing the signs of the time! Those who have ears to hear but do not listen, what catastrophic event awaits them. Oh, beloved, The Blessed Holy Spirit of the Lord speaks expressly: "Those who have ears to hear, let him hear what The Spirit says." *Shalom.*

Day 7

The Word of the Lord came to me: "Son of man, the Israelites are saying, 'The vision he sees is for many years from now, and he prophesies about the distant future.' Therefore say to them, This is what the Sovereign Lord says: None of My Words will be delayed any longer; whatever I say will be fulfilled, declares The Sovereign Lord."

Eze 12:26-28

Time's Up!

I once watched a movie entitled 'Enough,' which depicts a wife who was abused by her husband. She tortuously endured the verbal and physical abuse of her attacker. The abused woman became so tired of the suffering of her husband, she ran away from the matrimonial home and entered a period of training in self-defence.

God says enough is enough. For a long time, Almighty God has been warning people to repent of their sins and many continue to disregard and disrespect Him, but He must act. Mercy will one day evaporate, and time shall be no more. God will say, "Enough! Time is up!"

As you read this devotional, you do not know if you are reading for the last time. Truth is, the God who owns the future knows all about us and He knows when the 'plug must be pulled.' Our days are numbered, and only God knows when those numbers will play.

Each day we write our resume with the way we live. The choices we make, what we do, what we leave undone, what we say and think - each of these has great implications for our future destination. While man is partial and may operate contrary to a contract made, God is never partial, and He gives to everyone what they deserve.

My friend, you who do not know Jesus Christ as Lord and Saviour: This is your moment to repent of your sins and turn to the Lord. You have been hearing the Gospel for a long time, and God is calling you. Today might very well be the last time you are given the opportunity to repent and turn. My friend, please, surrender to the Lord as your time may very well be up soon!

Day 8

They have seduced My people, saying, "Peace, and there was no peace; and one built up a wall, and, lo, others daubed it with untempered mortar."

Eze 13:10b

Lies of The Prophets

Instead of listening and believing the words of God's prophet Ezekiel to correct their ways, most citizens of Israel chose to believe in lying prophets. Those liars told them whatever they wanted to hear to tickle their fancy.

Although deceived, they did not mind since they claimed to be happy in their situation. To them, what the lying prophets told them was all they needed to hear. Nothing else satisfied. They were so gravely deceived that it was their choice to accept lies rather than the truth.

Many today are of the same disposition as those Israelites of Ezekiel's time. They want a watered-down gospel, a type of prosperity gospel, unsound doctrines that make them feel good and tickle their fancy, instead of the real substance of the Word of God. Today, many Christians are deceived by the voice of lying prophets/messengers who claim they have the message of God. However, some of these so-called prophets' bottom line is money.

Have you ever noticed that some preachers' chief message is about money and not about the crucified Christ? They do not preach about the wages of sin, neither do they preach about the gift of eternal life, but all about money and how to get rich. Yet, many are their listeners because such a message is about feeling good. Oh, beloved, many are drawn to doctrines of demons and highly unsound doctrines just because of their itching ears and unstable characters.

God is calling us all to soundness of doctrine. He wants us to get to the Bible and to know Him for ourselves. The time has come for Christians who have been solely relying upon people to stop doing that, and start relying on God Himself. It is time for some to stop running after people seeking 'a word,' as some who are being sought after are liars and grabbers of money. God has all the answers for our situations, so let us seek Him.

Do not listen to the false prophets who promise grand things when God is clearly saying, "Destruction is at hand." Do not be deceived — it will be to your own detriment.

Day 9

That I may take the house of Israel in their own heart, because they are all estranged from Me through their idols.

Eze 14:5

For the Love of Idols: Exposing the Secret Heart of an Estranged Wife

Israel's bitter behaviour of divorcing God for idols which they loved dearly proved to be their destruction. They turned from Almighty God and became intimate lovers with idols, and yet at the same time, they inquired of God as if they were still yoked together with Him.

God, however, unveiled the secrets of their puny hearts and exposed them to punishment. Yes, their hearts were far from Almighty God, and He answered their hearts by giving them what they desired. He gave them over to their idols because their hearts were estranged from Him for the love of idols. So sad indeed!

The love for idols is seen every day. Many have backslid from the pathway of truth to serve idols. Their love for idolatry has driven them from the truth to embrace a dangerous lifestyle of putting something or someone else in the place of Almighty God.

My friends, let us at all times put God first place since that is the only place He accepts and deserves. He will never settle for another place in our lives. He wants all of us, not only a part. When Jesus Christ died for us, He gave His all so we can have the fullness of His life inside us.

If you are not serving Him in total submission, you are involved in idol worship and clearly, in such a state, no one can truly love Him as He should be. In God's Book, no one can serve two masters at the same time. Also, no one can have one foot in God's Kingdom and the other in Satan's.

As Christians, may we be completely sold out to Him. Let not our hearts develop strange likings for idolatry. If that happens, we may eventually become estranged from our God.

Day 10

Therefore this is what the Sovereign Lord says: "As I have given the wood of the vine among the trees of the forest as fuel for the fire, so will I treat the people living in Jerusalem. I will set My face against them. Although they have come out of the fire, the fire will consume them and when I set My face against them, you will know that I Am The Lord. I will make the land desolate because they have been unfaithful," declares The Sovereign Lord.

Eze 15:6-8

Judgement Is Unavoidable

When the wickedness of a nation reaches its full maturity, nothing can stop the judgement of God from being exacted upon that nation. The judgement of God can take various forms, but the result must be extensive suffering and untold losses.

Israel had to pay dearly for her actions because of the multitude of sins committed without repentance. Their worst sin was idolatry - spiritual adultery. This was a great insult to Almighty God who was a Husband to them. Whenever one revels in such an activity, there is really no place for God. And with almost an entire country sweeping at full pace in idolatry? What will God do? Will He not act? Surely, He must! Israel was judged by God for the sins of idolatry and if one continues in sin without repenting, judgement is ascertained.

What is happening in Jamaica today? Is our island facing judgement? Idolatry is at an all-time high in our nation. People, in general, do not want God and it is reflected in their behaviour. They love to worship idols and God is only enquired of when in deep need. Look at the levels of corruption in successive governments and many governmental institutions, the high number of scandalous events and the lack of Godly spiritual values. The murder rate for such a small nation continues to spiral out of control and it continues to be sin and more sin. Will God not act — or is He already showing signs of judgment in Jamaica?

Yes, many believe that since we are living in a dispensation of grace, there is a licence to sin. God forbid! Grace is here, but God expects us to be holy.

To live in sin is a disrespect to God. Furthermore, when sin becomes a way of life without remorse, grace is very much frustrated. When the grace of God is frustrated then God continues to take note and a nation, or an individual may experience God's judgement. Truth is, there is a price to pay.

Dearly beloved, may we endeavour to please Almighty God, irrespective of those who see it fit to oppose Him. Also, let us intercede on behalf of this nation that is in deep spiritual crisis, remembering that if the cup is full, judgement is unavoidable.

Day 11

On the day you were born your cord was not cut, nor were you washed with water to make you clean, nor were you rubbed with salt or wrapped in cloths. No one looked at you with pity or had compassion enough to do any of these things for you. Rather, you were thrown out into the open field, for on the day you were born you were despised. Then I passed by and saw you kicking about in your blood, and as you lay there in your blood, I said to you, Live!

I made you grow like a plant of the field. You grew up and developed and became the most beautiful of jewels. I bathed you with water and washed the blood from you and put ointments on you. However, you trusted in your beauty and used your fame to become a prostitute. You lavished your favours on anyone who passed by and your beauty became his.

Eze 16:4-7a, 9 & 15

Lest We Forget

Chapter sixteen of Ezekiel declares God as a Husband in deep lament over the unfaithfulness of His wife Israel. God recalled how He was faithful to her. He spoke of when Israel was rejected and how He took her in, cleaned her up, and grew her from infancy to magnificent beauty. He then entered a covenant relationship of deep intimacy with her. In response, Israel instead dissed her Husband.

Israel did not remember God's love and His faithfulness but wholly gave herself over to prostitution. She used what her Husband gave her to beautify herself and lavished it upon her lovers. She committed adultery with not just one partner, but several. Israel dissed God. Oh, what pain and sadness endured by the Faithful Husband!

Is there any difference today? Many who had no job prayed and begged God for one. Some even wept as they expressed faithfulness toward God. But, as soon as God gave the job, things changed. The once faithful Christian who loved the church and God's work now has no time to go to church. Work and money have become the priority. Has God given you the life partner you asked for, and more time is now devoted to your partner and family, rather than to God? Is it possible that one has so much that God can no longer fit in the picture? You are elevated in your job and getting more money, but have you been paying your tithes? Remember, it is not all that we earn which belongs to us. Let us not make the callous mistake of robbing the Lord's money. There is always a penalty for stealing.

Blessed people of God, let us never turn our backs on Jesus. He did it all for us. Let us never forget what He did for us when He died upon the cross for our sins. We were so filthy in sin, but it was Jesus who washed us in His blood and made us clean. He loves us with endless, passionate love, and each day He sustains us. Yes, we are cared for, protected, kept, guided, and provided for. We can continue to speak of His goodness to us in so many ways. Lest we turn from Him and forget His love to us, may He once more lead us to Calvary. Therefore, beloved, let us never diss our Covenant Partner, Jesus Christ.

It is a tragedy to forget Almighty God. He loved Israel dearly and He loves us just the same. Israel was lavished with His beauty but turned away from Him and paid the price for being unfaithful. We too are lavished with His blessings. Let us instead get closer to Him and serve Him with all our spirit, soul, and body.

Day 12

"All the trees of the field will know that I The Lord bring down the tall tree and make the low tree grow tall. I dry up the green tree and make the dry tree flourish. I The Lord have spoken, and I will do it."

Eze 17:24

Whomever He Pleases

The Lord used a parable to make a critical point to the Israelites. On several occasions, God used this tool to call attention to a point and to communicate His thoughts to His people.

Israel forfeited her position in God, as well as her possession from God. Still, God had the last word — Israel was cut down. God brought down Israel due to her high level of unrepentant idolatry. She was well positioned in God, having all the blessings that other countries longed for with great envy. Israel, however, traded these certain blessings for idols.

In Ezekiel's day, God cut down the tree of Israel. Because of the unrepentant sins that many today are revelling in, God is still cutting down trees. God cuts down those whom He sees fit for cutting and He sets up those whom He chooses.

My friend, you do not have to lower your standards to get favours. Many Christians are where they are because of indulgence in spiritual adultery. Some have given up their dignity and have laid down sexually with a manager or leading figure just to be favoured. The constant tale-bearing, news-carrying, backbiting and silent assassination of a colleague or church member just to be elevated to a position is sickening to the Lord.

As you serve the Lord, some around you are involved in idolatry just to get by. Do not partake of their actions. Do not follow them. Just bloom right where you are and grow in Almighty God. When you are faithful to God and it seems you are stagnating or are being overlooked by your superiors, do not worry. God will set you up as you remain faithful to Him.

Remember this, He sets up one and cuts down another.

Day 13

"The soul who sins is the one who will die. The son will not share the guilt of the father, nor will the father share the guilt of the son. The righteousness of the righteous man will be credited to him, and the wickedness of the wicked will be charged against him. Do I take any pleasure in the death of the wicked?" Declares The Sovereign Lord. "Rather, Am I not pleased when they turn from their ways and live?"

Eze 18:20 & 23

The Responsibility Rests with the One Who Sins

Sin always looks to pass on responsibility. Many commit sins and then blame others for their wrongdoing. However, when one sins, he or she is responsible for the behaviour.

God warned Israel that the sins of the father will not bring punishment to the son if the son walked uprightly, and vice versa. He knew that sin causes separation from Him as it opposes His very nature. Furthermore, because sin is a deterrent and seriously aggressive to righteousness, God has put measures in place to grant persons the power to overcome sin.

Sin's presence in the world is the reason Jesus Christ came to save us from its power and penalty. Consequently, no one must live in sin, nor should sin dominate anyone. Sin should never be a master over anyone because Jesus Christ gave His life to set people free. Clearly, no one has any excuse to live in sin, since sin causes separation from God Almighty who is holy.

Living in sin has grave consequences, but worst of all is when someone dies in sin. The awful result is spiritual damnation — straight into Hell.

My friends, you who have not accepted Jesus Christ as Lord and Saviour, your life seriously opposes Jesus Christ. You are lost and heading straight into Hell, the Lake of Fire. The time is now for you to change your direction. You see, friends, sin may be appealing and attractive, but it is very dangerous. It breeds restlessness and peacelessness into the souls of humans and a state of profane war in their spirits. To be held as a prisoner of sin is a serious catastrophe, but you do not have to remain under the bondage of sin's domain.

Do you want to serve God Almighty with all your heart and to escape the penalty and power of sin?

Jesus Christ is calling you to come to Him. Stop making excuses and turn to the Lord who loves you and is willingly ready to save you. Here in St Matthew 11:28-30, Jesus gave the timely invitation to lost souls:

"Come to Me, all you who are weary and burdened, and I will give you rest. Take My yoke upon you and learn from Me, for I am gentle and humble in heart, and you will find rest for your souls. For My yoke is easy and My burden is light."

Friend, are you are tired of living in sin? Tired of serving the Devil? Do you want to be delivered? Pray this simple prayer below by faith to Almighty God. He will immediately save you and set you free.

Dear Heavenly Father, I am a sinner and separated from You. I know that only You have the power to save me, and I need You to save me. Lord, I come to You today in the precious name of

Jesus Christ. Your Word in John 6:37 reveals, *"Him that cometh to Me, I will in no wise cast out."* So, Lord, I humbly come to You, and I know You will not cast me away. In Romans 10:9-10 the Word states, *"If you confess with your mouth, Jesus is Lord, and believe in your heart that God has raised Him from the dead, you will be saved. For it is with the heart that you believe and are justified, and it is with your mouth that you confess and are saved."*

Therefore, Lord upon the profession of Your Word, I believe that Jesus Christ is Lord. I believe that He came to earth, being human, and died upon the cross to save me from my sins. With my heart, I believe He is the Son of God; and with my mouth, I confess that He is Lord.

Lord, I know that only the blood of Your Son Jesus Christ has the power to wash away my sins. As I confess Jesus Christ as Lord and confess my sins to you, I ask You to please forgive me of all the sins I have committed against You, knowingly and unknowingly. Make me clean. Make me Your child.

Thank You, Lord, for forgiving me and for giving me the power over sin. Now, Lord, please fill me with Your blessed Holy Spirit. Lead me to live a victorious life, pleasing You in all that I think, speak, and do. I pray in Jesus' name. *Amen.*

Day 14

With hooks they pulled him into a cage and brought him to the king of Babylon. They put him in prison, so his roar was heard no longer on the mountains of Israel.

Eze 19:9

The Roar of the Once Mighty Lion Ceased

Have you ever noticed how afraid some persons are of others because of their behaviour? Their voices are like poison to the ears of their hearers. In the eyes of some of these persons, they are in control and are not accountable to anyone. As the old saying goes, 'Wen big man talk, no dog bark.' Many of these loud and insensitive individuals are so full of themselves and are crowned with pride.

Years ago, Hitler ruled Germany. The tyrant was Austrian by birth but became a German citizen, and in 1933, he rose to the helm of power in Germany, becoming its Chancellor. In August 1934, he rose to the status of Führer — the absolute dictator of Germany. Hitler was selfish and his ambition was to rule the world. However, his quest was to slaughter all Jewish people.

The ghastliest events ever experienced by the world came from his wicked and selfish behaviour. The early to mid-1940s saw World War Two which claimed the lives of an estimated fifty to ninety million people. The same war was started by Hitler's ideology. He brainwashed millions of Germans to believe they were an Aryan race and that they were far superior to other races. He treated many with great disdain with his fascist leadership and he roared in Europe. Many throughout the world were afraid of this insane man, but he eventually met his demise and his roaring ceased.

Ezekiel's prophecy about Jehoiachin and his subsequent and swift demise was a direct consequence of God exacting judgement upon the leadership of Judah. A young king who came to the throne on December 9, 598 BCE, Jehoiachin reigned just three months and ten days in Jerusalem. Like some of his predecessors, he did evil in the eyes of the Lord. He inflicted unjust punishment upon regular Jews and caused them much pain and untold sufferings. He did not fear God. To hurt God and His people was a task of simplicity. His behaviour was on display and in full view of God. For this reason, God allowed him to be captured and carried off to Babylon. There he became a prisoner of Nebuchadnezzar, caged like an animal.

Years before, the prophet Jeremiah in chapter 22:28-30, prophesied about the doom and destruction of this same Jehoiachin:

"Is this man Jehoiachin a despised, broken pot, an object no-one wants? Why will he and his children be hurled out, cast into a land they do not know? O land, land, land hear the word of the Lord! This is what The Lord says: 'Record this man as if childless, a man who will not prosper in his lifetime, for none of his offsprings will prosper, none will sit on the throne of David or rule anymore in Judah.'"

God was tired of the wickedness of Judah's leaders. Jehoiachin would surely be destroyed, and his father's dynasty would certainly crumble. His reign of terror and roaring of disdain ended abruptly. He was captured and imprisoned in a foreign land where he was silenced.

Ezekiel viewed the nation of Judah as a lioness and the kings of Judah as lion cubs. They were wicked and oppressive to the subjects they were set over. Regular citizens of Judah lived in terror as they suffered under the hands of some selfish, disrespectful, and unkind leaders, who made their lives a living hell. Jehoiachin was a successor of his father's evil regime but became an object of God's judgement.

Today, many lions and lionesses are roaring in homes, churches, schools, workplaces, governments, and every conceivable sector of society. Some behave as if the world belongs to them, that persons must seek their permission to exist. Evil today has reached unprecedented levels, but God is making records.

To the leadership of Jamaica, government institutions, churches, workplaces, homes, and many other places: Almighty God has called us to lead with justice and fairness. Therefore, let us honour Him by doing so.

For years, many Jamaicans have experienced an oppressive style of leadership across the length and breadth of this nation. God has taken everything into account. He is concerned about what is happening and He will act.

To you leaders in diverse sectors who have made it your prime ambition to oppress your subjects, God is clearly documenting your actions. Watch it, you oppressors! Do you think God is blind to the ills and hurt you are causing? Do you think He is deaf to the cries of His beloved children whom you are oppressing? Your roaring will certainly be ended. If God did not save the kings of Israel and Judah because of the oppression of their subjects, who do you think you are, that you will get away? He will certainly act, and some of you might just be imprisoned by either man or God Himself!

Repent and turn to Almighty God and do what is right, and God will bless your leadership. The great prophet Micah in chapter 6:8 records, *"He has shown you, O mortal, what is good, and what does The Lord requires of you? To act justly and to love mercy and to walk humbly with your God."* That is what is required of us as leaders.

Day 15

You say, "We want to be like all the nations, like the peoples of the world, who serve wood and stone."

You are an Original

You are created in the image of Almighty God. Born of His Holy Spirit and washed in the precious blood of Jesus Christ, you are destined to be only like Him.

Israel looked at their neighbours who were worshippers of detestable idols and envied them. What a state of callousness! Israel was handpicked and chosen by God Himself. He protected and provided for them and made His abode among them. He sustained them and defended them against their enemies. They had the incomparable, undisputed, all-powerful God as their source, yet they were not satisfied. Israel wanted to be like their enemies. God, however, did not create them to be like their neighbours.

O, beloved, you do not have to try and fit in. That is not your place. Why do you think it a life-and-death situation to be like those in the world? You do not have to dress as they do, think as they do, or act as they do. You do not need to be accepted by them.

You were never designed to be like everyone else. You are an original.

Don't you know that you were called, separated, and appointed by and for God's use? Your body is the temple of the Holy Spirit. Do not soil your bodies through sexual sins. Those who dwell in sexual sins and are encouraging you to join in on the action do not love you. Their actions amount to idolatry. Stay away from those who are bringing you there.

Remember, you are specially created. You are an original, not a carbon copy. Do not try to fit in where you do not belong. Stay in Christ Jesus, your Authority. *Shalom.*

Day 16

The Word of The Lord came to me. "Son of man, set your face against Jerusalem and preach against the sanctuary. Prophesy against the land of Israel and say to her: This is what The Lord says: I Am against you. I will draw My sword from the scabbard and cut off from you both the righteous and the wicked."

Eze 21:1-3

I Am Against You

If Almighty God tells you that He is against you, you are in serious trouble. However, why would God be against anyone?

As was the case, Israel was His chosen nation who turned against Him and violated His commands by committing spiritual adultery. Yet, although He beckoned to them to turn from their idolatry, they refused, causing Him to act. Brothers and sisters, to every action, there is an equal and opposite reaction. They sinned indiscriminately against God and were unwilling to repent. As a result, God punished them.

God turns against an individual or a nation because of continuous sinning. Although He is entreating them to correct their ways, they refused. They turned a deaf ear to Him until the grace allotted to them dissipated and vanished.

"Why are you disrespecting Me?" says the Lord. God is saying this right now to many who continue to ignore Him. Don't you know that it is an act of disrespect to disregard the voice of God? You may say you have not heard Him speaking, but every time His servants witness to you about Him, He is speaking to you. At this moment, through this message, He is speaking to you. He is telling you to repent of your sins and turn to Him.

The truth is, friends, your time on Earth is limited and your days are numbered. Indeed, they are coming to their end. If, after reading this message, you continue in your sinful ways, you would once more ignore and disrespect Him. I assure you; God does not like it when anyone disrespects Him.

It is not His desire to turn against anyone, but sin opposes Him. If you are continuing in sin, you are opposing Him. Furthermore, anyone who continues in sin and refuses to repent will find himself or herself in trouble with God.

May these words from God - "I am against you" - never be a reality for you.

Day 17

Her officials within her are like wolves tearing their prey; they shed blood and kill people to make unjust gain. Her prophets whitewash these deeds for them by false visions and lying divinations. They say, this is what the Sovereign Lord says, when the Lord has not spoken. The people of the land practice extortion and commit robbery; they oppress the poor and needy and ill-treat the aliens, denying them justice.

Eze 22:27-29

The Scourge and Curse of Ill-Gotten Gain

Once, a Christian contractor was the frontrunner to be awarded a contract to repair a stretch of road. The contractor was, however, informed by an official that although the job values a certain sum, he should hike the cost by an extra eight million dollars. The extra money would belong to the official. The contractor did not accede to the official's request, citing that the request was morally and spiritually wrong. Consequently, he was not awarded the contract.

The making of unjust gain by a country's officials is not a new feature. Rather, it is an old, unscrupulous practice. During Ezekiel's days, officials in Israel created various avenues to make ill-gotten gains. They exploited the young, robbed from the poor and shed innocent blood in their bid to satisfy their unquenchable, disgusting greed. Those immoral officials sought out every way to make themselves rich at the expense of their subjects. They did not care who got hurt or killed. So evil!

To add insult to injury, those corrupt officials were supported in their wrongdoings by false prophets who claimed they heard from Almighty God. Those corrupt prophets were benefactors of the officials' unjust gains. The poor were made poorer as they were robbed and abused by the country's officials as well as others who extorted them. What a tragedy!

Does this sound familiar? If so, that's because history has a way of repeating itself.

In many countries, several citizens are suffering from ruthless, oppressive leaders who apply all kind of measures to squeeze every last thing out of them. People are overtaxed, extorted, and robbed by government officials whose pockets are ever filled. The masses of the people continue to get hungrier and poorer, while some unscrupulous politicians and their friends get richer at the expense of robbing poor people. What will they say to God when He confronts them?

One of the problems experienced in some countries is that some of the oppressed have no one to help them. It makes no sense to report their plight because no human listens. What is worse, some church leaders whom God has charged to speak against the ills that are done to the poor and the oppressed, are doing nothing. Some are afraid, while others are benefactors of unjust gains from these official thieves.

O, Christian brothers and sisters, there is a need to be filled: to minister to the needy. When Jesus calls and saves us, our lives are His. That means we belong to Him and need to do whatever He tells us to do. May we never close our eyes and ears to the needs of the oppressed; they need us. Extortion, robbery, and murder are happening around us. Let us, therefore, reach out to those oppressed as the Lord leads.

To all those officials who are involved in oppressing the poor and needy by extorting, robbing, and murdering them, and to those church leaders who support them in their wrongs, God sees and knows what you have done and are still doing. Rest assured: you will be exposed and judged. You have created a legacy of doom with your ill-gotten gains. A curse follows them, one that will affect your offspring. You, however, have a window of opportunity to come clean by confessing your evils. In sincerity, repent and beg God to forgive you. He is faithful to do it.

Day 18

The word of the Lord came to me: "Son of man, there were two women, daughters of the same mother. They became prostitutes in Egypt, engaging in prostitution from their youth. In that land their breasts were fondled and their virgin bosoms caressed. The older was named Oholah, and her sister was Oholibah. They were mine and gave birth to sons and daughters. Oholah is Samaria, and Oholibah is Jerusalem. Therefore, I handed her over to her lovers, the Assyrians, for whom she lusted. They stripped her naked, took away her sons and daughters and killed her with the sword. She became a byword among women and punishment was inflicted on her. Her sister Oholibah saw this, yet in her lust and prostitution she was more depraved than her sister."

Eze 23:1-4 & 9-10

Handed Over to their Lovers for the Assault

Under the leadership of Saul, David and then Solomon, Israel was one united nation. However, at the end of Solomon's reign in the year 931 BCE, civil war broke out in Israel. The one nation became divided into two separate countries in the year 930 BCE. To the north was Israel with its capital Samaria, otherwise called Oholah. To the south lay Judah with its capital Jerusalem. Jerusalem was also called Oholibah.

Both Oholah and Oholibah were siblings, having the same husband, Almighty God. However, they turned away from their caring husband to prostitution and refused to repent and return to their legitimate spouse. God was tired of their betrayal and adultery. As a result, He handed them over to their lovers, who punished and destroyed them.

Sin will surely destroy those who live in it and refuse to repent.

Backsliders, you are precariously positioned on a slippery slope heading towards an eternal hell. You were once bubbling for Christ. You loved Him dearly, being filled with such excitement for your lover. No one was closer to you than He. Truth is, He was your first love. To commune with Him was joy unspeakable and full of glory and your days beamed brightly. What has gone wrong? What have you done with your former lover? Have you sacrificed your loving conjugal relationship for an adulterous stance? Where is the passion that you once exhibited towards your Lover, Almighty God?

To those who once accepted Jesus Christ as Lord and Saviour and are living in a backslidden state, the call is for you to return to Him.

Although you have divorced your husband for another lover, do not follow the sad examples of the siblings Oholah and Oholibah. They turned from their lover and did not return after a long beckoning. They suffered for their adulterous lifestyles and were handed over to be punished by their adulterous partners. Their own sin destroyed them.

You do not have to continue on the slippery path of backsliding. If you continue and thereafter die in sin, you will suffer untold punishment. Truth is, if you repent of your sins and return to your former spouse, the Lord Jesus Christ, He will abundantly pardon and forgive you.

My friend, your life is at stake and your days are called to reckoning. You have this moment and this moment only. Make good use of it and humbly seek God's forgiveness. He Who loves you patiently awaits but the waiting will not be forever.

Day 19

The word of the Lord came again unto me, saying, "Son of man, set thy face against the Ammonites, and prophesy against them; and say unto the Ammonites, Hear the word of The Lord God; Thus saith The Lord God; because thou saidst, Aha, against My sanctuary, when it was profaned; and against the land of Israel, when it was desolate; and against the house of Judah, when they went into captivity. Behold, therefore I will deliver thee to the men of the east for a possession, and they shall set their palaces in thee, and make their dwellings in thee: they shall eat thy fruit, and they shall drink thy milk."

Eze 25:1-4

The Same Knife

Do you take pleasure in rejoicing over people's misfortune? Why gloat over another's downfall? Don't you know that the same misfortune that besets your neighbour can destroy you?

Israel and Judah did great evil in the eyes of God. Their disgusting adulterous lifestyle angered Him. They did not express remorse when the Prophet of God warned them, nor did they show any sign of slowing down from their wickedness. Consequently, God allowed them to suffer extensively.

Their neighbours the Ammonites did not take heed, nor did they humble themselves either. Instead, Ammon rejoiced over Israel's downfall. Yet, Almighty God would not allow anyone to gloat over and celebrate His estranged wife's downfall.

Not because one is found in an unfortunate situation, gives any reason to another to rejoice over his or her misfortune. Truth is that the same knife that kills the sheep also kills the goat. The same misfortune that befell one can visit another.

God has called us to be our brother's keeper. He does not expect us to rejoice over our brother's or sister's demise.

Be clear on this, it is not kind to rejoice because a man or a woman of God has fallen. God does not take kindly to anyone who gloats over any of His children's downfall. Instead, why not pray for the fallen and assist wherever necessary? Keep in mind that what has happened to your brother or sister may very well happen to you.

Day 20

In the eleventh year, on the first day of the month, the word of The Lord came to me: "Son of man, because Tyre has said of Jerusalem, Aha! The gate to the nations is broken, and its doors have swung open to me; now that she lies in ruins I will prosper, therefore this is what The Sovereign Lord says: I Am against you, O Tyre, and I will bring many nations against you, like the sea casting up its waves."

Eze 26:1-3

The Opportunist

"When a man is down, keep him down." This is an expression that is often used in sporting circles. In dominos, for example, one of the four participants will often face a streak of six losses in a row at the hand of one player. The other three will regularly work together and try to ensure he or she gets the "six-love" since he is already down.

The gates of Jerusalem were broken down and the city lay in utter ruin. It was total devastation being experienced by the people of Jerusalem. Yet, Tyre decided to make their lives even more miserable. Their plan was to enter through the broken-down gates and take whatever scraps were left. They were heartless.

Many people today are also heartless. They do not care what misfortune befalls another, so long as they can benefit. Have you ever noticed an accident where victims are suffering and needed help? Despite this, some on the scene just keep digging to see what they can find instead of assisting the needy. I have seen a cement truck overturned on a major thoroughfare. Passers-by merely pack cement away for themselves without any sense of care that someone needs help. Almighty God is against that type of uncaring behaviour. He who sees will certainly act.

Tyre's intention to prosper at Jerusalem's downfall was a serious mistake. Not because God had acted against His own people gave anyone the permission to disadvantage them. God's people are His possession. No one should profit illegally off them. He will act and will do it swiftly.

I, therefore, say this: May we not adopt the style of seeing a brother or sister down and push him or her further in the ground. Let us help. If God has assigned someone to us, He has given to us the capacity, talents, gifts and means to assist. Consequently, let us do what God expects of us and not disadvantage the needy.

Day 21

The word of the Lord came to me: "Son of man, take up a lament concerning Tyre, situated at the gateway to the sea, merchant of peoples on many coasts, This is what The Sovereign Lord says: You say O Tyre, 'I am perfect in beauty.'

The merchants among the nations hiss at you; you have come to a horrible end and will be no more."

Eze 27:1-3 & 36

Self-Praise Is No Recommendation

Tyre was a coastal city with a large portion of its wealth generated on the high seas. It was a significant city, as all the major nations of the day traded merchandise with her. Because of its imposing wealth and position close to the sea, the air about the city was filled with pride. The citizens of Tyre thought they were highly special since their country boomed economically. Consequently, they praised themselves for Tyre's so-called magnificent beauty. They never even gave God thanks for His blessings but instead praised their own effort. What a tragedy!

God knew that the attitude of Tyre's occupants was continually rife with pride, and He had to act. He ensured that the pride of Tyre became defunct; it was no more. God destroyed the once-booming, magnificent city of Tyre, in all its self-proclaimed beauty.

God hates pride. When pride takes hold of a person, an organization or a country, serious trouble looms.

Many are destroyed because of their lack of humility. They have allowed their position and possessions to fool them. It is clear today that some who have named the name of Jesus Christ have allowed what God has given them to become their god. What about the gifts and talents given to them by God? Indeed, beloved, after a while, the once-mighty prophet, evangelist, pastor, teacher, or singer is not seen or seldom heard from. Sometimes, the pride they exhibited has angered God and caused Him to act. Not because one has added some status to his or her name, or garnered a higher position in the job market, makes them more important than anyone else! Having more money or more influence does not cause God to see us on a different surface.

Friends, do not worship what you have. To worship something or someone other than the Almighty God is the most destructive mistake anyone can make. God does not accept rivals.

Tyre was filled with pride and praised herself because of her beauty. Is there any difference today? Many are deceived because of their beauty, education, company, position, or money. O, what a tragedy to worship the created and not the Creator! God will act!

Day 22

The word of the Lord came to me: "Son of man, say to the ruler of Tyre, This is what The Sovereign Lord says: In the pride of your heart you say, 'I am a god; I sit on the throne of a god in the heart of the seas,' but you are a man and not a god, though you think you are wise as a god."

Eze 28:1-2

Woe be Unto Those who Set Themselves Up as Gods!

O, what a fatal mistake for the one who takes on the status of a god! Such a perversion of behaviour is regularly seen in many homes, governments, churches, schools, workplaces, and many other sectors. At times one behaves as if he or she is a god and is ultimately in charge. It is only what he or she says that goes. What a pride! O, what a deception! The demon of pride is fully at work.

Have you ever noticed the prideful behaviour of some supervisors, managers, pastors, principals, government leaders and others in leadership positions? They behave as if they are high and mighty and only their decision matters for their organization. They express an attitude of perfection, violating their organization's norms and values for the benefit of themselves and their friends.

Some of these 'self-perfected' individuals can only feel empowered whenever they treat their subjects in the most demeaning and disrespectful ways. Their purpose is to dominate and make the lives of ordinary persons miserable. They treat people with contempt, regarding them lower than animals. These so-called gods beg people to worship them. Yet, God sees, and He is aware of what goes on. He knows the embarrassment and pain constantly borne by people under the leadership of those so-called gods. Be it resolutely clear: Almighty God defends the rights of the marginalized. He will disgrace and bring down those self-proclaimed gods who trouble His children.

The ruler of Tyre was filled with pride. He manifested a god-like status. He claimed that he was god and that his seat was the throne of a god. He was so disrespectful to Almighty God that he did not bother to acknowledge Him in anything. As far as he was concerned, his brilliant negotiating skills and great leadership ability brought success to Tyre. To him, he was his own god and accountable to no one.

He was so steep in pride and full of himself. He believed that defeat could not come his way. He was so wrapped up in himself, so filled with conceit in his god status, he did not believe that the day for his demise was imminent. He was deceived.

Woe unto those who have taken the place of Almighty God! Woe unto those who have set themselves up as gods in their churches, schools, workplaces, governments, and homes! God is calling you to repent and turn to Him. Your evil treatment of your subjects has not gone unnoticed. Your secret meetings and uncaring attitude have made you a target to Almighty God. He is presently aiming His arrow at you. You will be defeated and destroyed just like the ruler of Tyre who refused to acknowledge God and repent of his evils.

This is a warning to you, O self-proclaimed gods! Your sins have reached the nostrils of God. Humble yourselves, repent of your sins and turn to Almighty God with all your heart. Remember, your esteemed position has no power to save you. You must

Day 23

"Son of man set your face against Pharaoh king of Egypt and prophesy against him and against all Egypt. Speak to him and say: This is what The Sovereign Lord says: I Am against you, Pharaoh king of Egypt, you great monster lying among your streams. You say, the Nile is mine; I made it for myself. I will leave you in the desert, you and all the fish of your streams. You will fall on the open field and not be gathered or picked up. I will give you as food to the beasts of the Earth and the birds of the air."

Eze 29:2-3 & 5.

Was it Yours from the Beginning?

The spirit of greed has taken over the lives of many who are not satisfied with what God has given them. They rob, destroy, and kill to satisfy their destructive, craving appetites.

The South China Sea has been a sore point in the last few years. Several countries border the same sea. Some of these countries have laid heavy claim to one of the world's busiest sea lanes. Furthermore, the South China Sea is believed to be rich in natural gas and crude oil. It is also estimated that about five trillion dollars' worth of international trade passes through that body of water every year. Countries have staked their claim over the Sea to control its high economic value. In a bid to own the Sea, some of the bordering countries have even reclaimed lands from it. They have made islands and have set up buildings on them.

However, China has claimed about ninety per cent of the huge waterway. It is alleged that they have reclaimed more land from the water body than any other country. It is further asserted that China has militarized the man-made islands. They threaten any foreign ships passing close to what they now call China's property. A few months ago, China's president, Xi Jinping claimed that the South China Sea belongs exclusively to China. He declared that China will not give up one inch of its territory. O, what greed on display! These actions have led to conflict and confusion. The truth is, when you are greedy enough to want all, then you will lose all. The South China Sea belongs to God.

Similarly, Pharaoh laid claim to a major historic waterway and an important river known as the Nile. The Great River Nile is filled with resources for the benefit of regular citizens. However, the most important element provided to Egyptians of old was fertile land, since a vast portion of Egypt is desert. Along the Nile's bank, the soil is so rich and produces a variety of crops.

Pharaoh, however, believed that the country of Egypt and the river flowing through it was his, that they were his creation. His whole posture and behaviour angered Almighty God. Pharoah's attitude did not go down well with the One True God who owns the Nile River and the land of Egypt. As a result, God was adamant that He would judge Pharoah for his actions and He did.

Why do some lay claim to God's Church? Some have placed their names on God's property, behaving as if they are the sole owners. Can you believe that only at their behest can any enter as a member? Not to mention, when God Almighty decrees that some things are to be done in the church, certain activities cannot take place unless the so-called 'church owners' give permission. What a tragedy for the one who sees it fit to stand against Almighty God!

Beloved, some not only lay claim to God's church here. They also claim to permit entrance to Heaven or Hell. So many are stumbling blocks in the church because they claim ownership of God's property. But God will certainly judge them if they refuse to repent. Some churches can only thrive when God removes the stumbling blocks. It is God's church.

May we always remind ourselves that the church is not owned by anyone, but by God Himself. We are members of God's eternal church. Our wonderful edifices here are no match to our position in Jesus. Let us be clear that we will certainly leave these edifices behind. We do not own God's church, so let us function well as lively stones and not lay claim to God's property.

Day 24

This is what The Sovereign Lord says: "I will put an end to the hoarders of Egypt by the hand of Nebuchadnezzar king of Babylon. He and his army, the most ruthless of nations will be brought in to destroy the land. They will draw their swords against Egypt and fill the land with the slain. I will dry up the streams of the Nile and sell the land to evil men; by the hand of foreigners I will lay waste the land and everything in it. I The Lord have spoken."

Eze 30:10-12

Handed Over to Foreigners!

Due to the level of irreverent behaviour and lack of respect towards God in Egypt by regular citizens and leaders, God handed the entire country of Egypt over to a most notorious man, King Nebuchadnezzar. It was God's will to allow King Nebuchadnezzar to raid Egypt and lay it to waste. Egypt incurred the anger of God to exact punishment against her. The whole nation thus suffered the wrath of Nebuchadnezzar and his invading army.

The sins of a nation can bring the judgement of God and cause the whole country to suffer. When leaders of a nation have no fear of God, the country has a serious problem. When a government is corrupt, it is likely that the corruption will filter down into many departments and organizations. In general, people will do what they choose to do. Sin will be sin, and to some, it is no problem. What was once morally wrong is now considered relative. People generally do not want Almighty God. They instead choose to live to please the flesh.

A highly corrupt country without penitence will always be an object of God's wrath. He will give His warnings through His prophets, but if there is no repentance, then the consequences of actions will be suffering.

Oftentimes, God uses a nation to punish another. One such method of punishment is to give up the country's rights to another nation. It is not good for a nation to sell most or all its major assets to foreign nations. However, because of corruption and unrepentant sins, God will hand over a country to another that will take control of it.

What about the invasion of certain foreign nations in a country or region? Could this be God signalling judgement? Some arrive with a plan of economic growth, saying it is to benefit the receiver. Yet in truth, in a few years from now, what will remain for the descendants of the receiving nation? When clearly checked, almost everything is owned by a foreign power.

At times God may punish a nation using invaders with weapons of destruction. This is what happened with Egypt. However, an invasion does not necessarily mean entering with guns and artilleries. The invading country can enter with money and economic clout coupled with deceit. They will buy out and take over. That is done at times to the detriment of a nation that has turned from Almighty God.

In days to come, some independent countries may just become colonies of a larger country.

Nebuchadnezzar was used by God to punish the Egyptians and to take control of their country. Many citizens suffered and a great number was killed. The Babylonians occupied the land of Egypt, perhaps the worst of all.

Day 25

"I will set fire to Egypt; Pelusium will writhe in agony. Thebes will be taken by storm; Memphis will be in constant distress. The young men of Heliopolis and Bubastis will fall by the sword, and the cities themselves will go into captivity. Dark will be the day of Tahpanhes when I break the yoke of Egypt; there her proud strength will come to an end. She will be covered with clouds, and her villages will go into captivity. So I will inflict punishment on Egypt, and they will know that I Am The Lord."

Eze 30:16-19

Why are So Many of our Young People Being Killed?

One of the ways a nation is seen to be under judgement is the wanton and senseless slaying of scores of children and young people. There is no more value in life - people just kill for no apparent reasons, and the fear of God is gone. A one-month-old infant in the arms of her mother is killed without hesitation by some old disgusting thugs.

Pelusium, Thebes, Memphis, Heliopolis, Bubastis and Tahpanhes were all ancient Egyptian cities. They drove Egypt's economy. The residents of those cities made up a sizeable portion of Egypt's population and many youths shared residence in them. The cities were strategically positioned both for commercial and spiritual activities. In fact, much of Egyptian trading was done in those cities. However, worshipping of idols was critical to the existence of the cities' populace, or so they thought. They saw idol worship as a mainstay and the practice was widespread and magnified. Contrastingly, the recognition of Almighty God was a no-no.

In God's judgement via Nebuchadnezzar, all those cities were gravely impacted. God ensured that the young men of Heliopolis and Bubastis met a violent end.

Friends, if our young people are being slaughtered indiscriminately like animals, it is an indication that judgement has begun upon our land. Are we taking note of what is happening to our young people today? Many of them do not want to go to church anymore! Many have no respect for their parents and other persons. Some hate God and the church and whatever it stands for. Some are so wrapped up in satanic activities. Their ambition is to create as much havoc as possible. Some take pride in discharging illegal firearms and they are not afraid of committing heinous murder.

Many of the youths in Heliopolis were steadfast in evil like their seniors. God judged them by allowing them to be brutally murdered.

Why are so many of Jamaica's young people being savagely slaughtered? Could it be a sign of God judging our nation? Let us view carefully and take heed!

Day 26

In the twelfth year, on the fifteenth day of the month, the word of The Lord came to me. "Son of man, wail for the hordes of Egypt and consign to the Earth below both her and the daughters of mighty nations, with those who go down to the pit. Say to them, Are you more favoured than others? Go down and be laid among the uncircumcised. You too O Pharaoh, will be broken and will lie among the uncircumcised, with those killed by the sword."

Eze 32:17-19 & 28

You May Get Away from Man, but Not from God!

For all his life, Pharaoh had disrespected Almighty God. He thought he was untouchable, special, and above reproach. He was a law unto himself since, in Egypt, he reigned supreme. He was a god amongst his people, considered immortal. Worship from Egypt's citizens was ascribed unto him. In fact, Egyptians were not allowed to worship anyone above their Pharaoh. Pharaoh's disrespectful attitude towards God was always on display, and God used Nebuchadnezzar to destroy him. It appeared that Pharaoh never read the annals of the kings of Egypt. Almighty God disgraced and decimated his predecessor, sending him to his watery grave in the Red Sea.

Embedded in Egyptian and Hebrew history is a record of an event where Almighty God delivered the Israelites from Egypt. The Israelites were slaves for hundreds of years in Egypt, held against their will. Their deliverance by God was so spectacular: although Israel was freed, Pharaoh, his men, chariots, horses, and other weapons were destroyed. God drowned them in the Great Red Sea (Sea of Reeds).

Today, many leaders have become a law unto themselves, doing just as they like. For them, being in leadership is all about their selfish ambition, not about the interest of their followers. Too many have become wealthy at the expense of their subjects, with their followers stricken in poverty. So many Pharaohs are at different levels of leadership in our society. Pharaohs big and small are making people's lives miserable.

To those unconscionable leaders who rule with evil intent and disrespect towards people, take note! You may be favoured by some men, worshipped, and treated in high esteem because of your title and position. Yet, God will treat you no differently than He treated all those who disrespected Him and refused to repent.

Yes, disrespectful leaders, you are displeasing God Almighty. You need to come to your senses and start doing what is right. O, unscrupulous leaders, in whatever field you lead, your works are on full display before Almighty God. He is calling you to repent of your iniquities and to turn to Him. He will abundantly pardon you if you seek His forgiveness.

Do you think you are so special to Him that He will overlook all your unrepentant behaviour? If you think so, you are dead wrong! Pharaoh and others, though special to man they were, felt the wrath of Almighty God. You are no different! Repent and turn to Almighty God before it is too late.

Day 27

The word of The Lord came to me: "Son of man, speak to your countrymen and say to them: when I bring the sword against a land, and the people of the land choose one of their men and make him their watchman, and he sees the sword coming against the land and blows the trumpet to warn the people, then if anyone hears the trumpet but does not take warning and the sword takes his life, his blood will be on his own head."

Eze 33:1-4

Your Blood Will Not be on My Head

At times I wondered, why has the Lord led me to prepare these daily devotionals from the Book of Ezekiel? The thought came to me that, just as God spoke to the nations during Ezekiel's time, judgement is either imminent or already here. People need to repent and turn to the Lord as these are serious times.

Beloved, I will only write and present what God asks of me. What He has been saying is relevant. It must not be taken lightly. We are responsible for whatever He presents to us. He speaks today through His Word and His people. Listen and follow what He asks.

Today, if you do not know Jesus Christ as Lord and Saviour, you are playing spiritual roulette with your life. You need to take stock of your life and repent of your sins. Willingly ask the Lord to use His blood and wash away your sins. You need help, and only He has the power to remove your sins. My friend, if you die in your sins, there is no two ways about where you will go. It will be nothing but a one-way ticket to Hell to be with Satan and his demons. Without repentance, you will be punished for all eternity.

63

If you are not saved and you are reading this devotional, you are responsible for what you are reading. Therefore, take heed! For if you die without accepting Jesus Christ, your blood will not be on my head.

Day 28

"Son of man, I have made you a watchman for the House of Israel; so hear the word I speak and give them warning from Me. When I say to the wicked, O wicked man, you will surely die, and you do not speak out to dissuade him from his ways, that wicked man will die for his sin, and I will hold you accountable for his blood."

Eze 33:7-8

Am I Accountable for His or Her Blood?

Fellow Christians, we are God's watchmen in this world. We were called, equipped, and sent to the lost of this world. We are charged to tell them that they need to repent of their sins and turn to Jesus Christ who will forgive them. Many unsaved persons are dying every day, making the no-return trip to a godless Hell. O, believers, won't we lead them to the Lord? The harvest is ripe, but few are the labourers.

The Israelites were steep in sin. They also proved extremely disrespectful to Almighty God, engaging in spiritual adultery. To worship idols was one of the worst insults Israel dished out to God. What a disgrace! Yet, despite the deepening disrespect towards God, He sent His servant Ezekiel to warn the Israelites to repent of their wrongdoings.

God called Ezekiel and employed him as a watchman. He was charged to warn the people of Israel to turn from their iniquities. As God's mouthpiece, he was expected to go to the people who rebelled against God. If the appointed watchman refused to do what God told him to do and persons died in their sins, he would have been responsible. Their blood would have rested upon his head. Such a situation may sound unfair, but it is not. Ezekiel was God's watchman and mouthpiece.

Similarly, we are God's watchmen and mouthpiece in this depraved world. We need to preach, teach, and prophesy to those in sin. Many want to preach, yes, but to whom? To a church filled with saved members? There are so many dying in sin! Many unsaved will not go to your church - they are on the streets, plazas, public places, workplaces and all over. Tell them that Jesus loves them and died for them! Tell them that if they turn to Him, repenting of their sins, He will forgive them.

Too many lazy Christians are in the church. These persons are merely satisfied that they are saved and have absolutely no concern for lost souls. They do not care if their own blood relative or next-door neighbour goes to Hell. They would never open their mouth to warn others to turn away from their sins. If you think that all you need to do is remain saved and nothing else, think again! You are making a serious mistake. Too many unsaved are around. Jesus has called, appointed, and equipped us with His Holy Spirit to go on the byways, roads, edges and everywhere to bid sinners to Him.

It is of utmost importance that no one loses his or her soul into Hell on account of us. If we are called to witness the Word of God to someone and did not and subsequently, that person dies without accepting Jesus Christ as Lord and Saviour, we are responsible for that person's soul in Hell. Their blood is upon our head. We are therefore in trouble with the Lord. O, many called themselves Christians but have turned people away from Almighty God with their hypocritical lifestyle. They say they are saved but their lifestyle opposes that of Christ's. Don't you know that we are watched by the world? Repent!

My beloved brothers and sisters, the time is now that we make it a priority to win the lost at any cost. The world needs us, Christians. We are God's mouthpiece in this generation and God is depending on us. May we never allow any to go to Hell because we did not do as the Lord has commanded. I do not want another's blood to rest upon my head. Do you?

Day 29

"Son of man, say to the House of Israel, This is what you are saying: 'Our offences and sins weigh us down, and we are wasting away because of them. How then can we live?' Say to them, as surely as I live, declares The Sovereign Lord, I take no pleasure in the death of the wicked, but rather that they turn from their ways and live. Turn! Turn from your evil ways! Why will you die, O House of Israel?"

Eze 33:10-11

A Chance to Live

Many people in the nation of Israel were tired of their sinful lifestyle. They knew they were alienated from God. Their stenchful lives before Him had attracted His wrath.

God loved the Israelites dearly and longed for fellowship with them. He missed intimacy with them. He, therefore, extended the call for them to return. He stretched out the olive branch to them. He gave them the choice to return or die in their sins. Clearly, God does not like when one dies in sin. He knows the pain, separation and regret that awaits him or her. For this reason, God offered each one a chance to live.

Today, He makes the same call to you who are living in sin. He is calling you, O man, woman, boy and girl. It is your time to accept the call. The call is urgent! The call is solemn! The call is personal! The call is for you! Every time you hear the call, if you reject it, you continue to reject Jesus Christ.

Jesus Christ is calling you by your name. You are special to Him. He loves you. He wants you to give your life to Him. He is calling you through His Word, His church, children, situations, and even through nature. He is begging you to turn from your sins and come to Him, where you will receive life everlasting.

My unsaved friends, you are living in deep trouble on the slopes of death. Jesus Christ is giving you another chance to turn from your sins to Him. He does not take pleasure in the death of sinners. He now offers you life. Seek the Lord before it is too late. Will you accept the call today? It is urgent!

Day 30

"If I (God) say to the wicked man, 'You will surely die,' but he then turns away from his sin and does what is just and right, if he gives back what he took in pledge for a loan, returns what he has stolen, follows the decree that gives life, and does no evil, he will surely live; he will not die. None of the sins he has committed will be remembered against him. He has done what is just and right; he will surely live."

Eze 33:14-16

Remembered No More

How wonderful it is for a convict before the human court to hear the judge say, "You are admonished and discharged, and the conviction is not recorded."

Israel's sins were gravely disrespectful to God. Yet, although their insurmountable evils reached unprecedented levels, God still loved them unconditionally. No measure or level of sin could stop God from loving them. He loved and cared for His estranged wife. He entreated her to return to Him. He was willing to write off the wrongs and not to record them against her. Blessed be the God of Love!

My unsaved friends, you may believe that your sins are too much for God to remove. You have done heinous acts against God and man. You have done criminal activities and because of your criminal acts, society has written you off. Your family has deserted you and rejection has taken you over. You are tired of your lifestyle and you now cry out for help and acceptance. God loves you and He is saying to you, *"Come unto Me, all ye who are laboured and are heavy laden and I will give you rest."* Your sins are not too much for God.

The prison door of sin is opened for you to escape. Jesus now stands at your door wanting to make an entrance and so He knocks. He just wants you to let Him in.

Friend, Jesus Christ loves you more than you may ever know. No one has ever loved you the way He does. He opens His arms to you, wanting you to receive His forgiveness.

No matter the degree of your sins or their magnitude, the blood of Jesus Christ can remove them. He will make you clean. His word echoed by the Apostle Paul in 2 Corinthians 5:17 states,

> "Therefore, if anyone is in Christ, you are a new creature. The old has gone and the new has come."

He wants to make you new. Will you make the exchange today: The old sinful state for the new regenerated life? Come to Jesus.

Day 31

"Yet, O House of Israel, you say, 'The way of The Lord is not just.' However, I will judge each of you according to his own ways."

Eze 33:20

Every Tub Has to Sit on its Own Bottom

Each of us, whether a person, group, or entity, must take responsibility for our own actions. There are certain things that we alone can do for ourselves, that we alone can take care of. Therefore, certain reactions accompany certain behaviours. Although in this life one can be punished for another's wrong actions, in God's Book, each one will receive a just reward for his or her own actions.

God pulled out all the stops in calling Israel back to Himself. Still, many of those He beckoned to did not want Him and thus refused Him, to their own peril. They got what they worked for, well paid for their unrepentant behaviour.

In Romans 6:23, the Apostle Paul posited,

> "For the wages of sin is death, but the gift of God is eternal life through Jesus Christ our Lord."

Paul indicated that each action will merit its payment. Sin has its wage or payment and that is eternal death. One who lives and dies in sin has no one to blame for going to Hell but him or herself.

God extended the olive branch to the House of Israel for her to return to Him. Instead, she blamed God and claimed that He was unjust. The people of Israel did not want to take responsibility for their own actions but blamed someone else for their behaviour. Is that indicative of what is happening today in every sector of society?

Instead of taking responsibility for their bad behaviour, many have blamed others for their own demise. Some, because of a spirit of pride will never apologize to someone they hurt but will find someone or something to blame. O, what a tragedy!

Although some will receive a just reward in this earthly life for their actions, others are not treated per their actions. However, before God, everyone will receive his or her just reward. No matter how close we are to our family and friends, the time will come when we must stand before God—and it will be singularly! God will deal with everyone independently of the other. 'Every tub will have to sit on its own bottom.'

Do you expect to continue to hurt people without consequence? Think again! Do you expect to continue to reject God, His Word, His church, and His servants and get away scot-free? If that is your belief, you are dead wrong! To every action, there is an equal and opposite reaction. God rewards everyone, both the just and the unjust.

Day 32

"Ye stand upon your sword, ye work abomination, and ye defile every one his neighbour's wife: and shall ye possess the land? Say thou thus unto them, thus saith The Lord God; As I live, surely they that are in the wastes shall fall by the sword, and him that is in the open field will I give to the beasts to be devoured, and they that be in the forts and in the caves shall die of the pestilence."

Eze 33:26-27

You Who Live by The Sword!

The people of Israel believed that they could do whatever they want. They believed nothing could cause them to lose their inheritance in Abraham. Oh, no! They were badly mistaken.

During Ezekiel's time, the people of Israel saw themselves as the apple of God's eyes. To them, they were so special since their forefather Abraham was God's friend. This was how they came to know about the promised land of Canaan that they were living on. That land was promised to Abraham and his descendants. Being firmly planted on that land, they surmised that nothing or no one could move them, irrespective of their attitude or behaviour. They believed that they belonged and had a right to be protected and provided for by God. Thus, they did not care how they lived.

The extent of evil that permeated the land was unprecedented. Abomination was an everyday occurrence. People were not afraid to perform any acts of sexual lewdness and other acts of immorality. Defiling a neighbour's wife sexually was just the norm. 'A nuh nutten dat.' Yet, they believed that God should have just allowed them to continue in their profanity and not disturb their inheritance.

But God is holy and cannot be mocked.

Those Israelites lived by the sword of unholiness and thus they were destroyed by the sword. They were destroyed by foreigners and booted out of their God-given inheritance.

Today, the cycle continues. Many do evil in various quarters and expect God to bless them. Some attack their neighbours with their viperous tongues and do all manner of evil, just to stay on top or to tear others down. In some workplaces, just to get promoted is a dogfight. A brother or a sister becomes no more but an enemy in the bid to be favoured. Therefore, the tongue is used to destroy another's character. O, some people deem it alright to slander another. However, that same sword will enter the mouth of the slanderer and effectively destroy him or her. Such an individual must reap what he or she has sown.

What about those who feel it is alright to tell professional lies about a co-worker? Yes, some supervisors sit with other workers and destructively rip apart other workers. They scandalize and demoralize another's character just to elevate their selfish ego. Ah, beloved, some behave as if they are indispensable, but they are so wrong. Some of them are the biggest liabilities in the workplace, yet they claim to be in control. What a deception! The methods they use against other staff members shall be used against them. God is still awake.

If your ambition is to spear others with your snaked tongue and slithering actions, there is no way you will get away. You have done plenty in secret, but God will expose you openly.

You wickedly used the sword against those amongst you, but the sword will come upon your own neck. Your passion for slaying your neighbour with your tongue and vandalising his or her character will 'dagger' your own heart. You will be haunted by your own actions. When it happens to you, do not blame anyone else for your demise. Blame yourself. You lived by the sword — what then did you expect? Shall you not also die by the sword?

Day 33

"My people come to you, as they usually do, and sit before you to listen to your words, but they do not put them into practice. With their mouths they express devotion, but their hearts are greedy for unjust gain. Indeed, to them you are nothing more than one who sings love songs with a beautiful voice and play an instrument well, for they hear your words but do not put them into practice.

Eze 33:31-32

Listen, But Do Not Follow

The Israelites claimed they wanted to hear the word of God from Ezekiel. They sat with the prophet, but they were not interested in what he had to say. Their hearts were so greedy, deeply embedded in unjust gain. Ezekiel informed them of the truth of God, of how they were to live, but they did not practice what was preached.

The word of God is preached, prophesied, and taught daily. Still, many who hear have no interest in what is said. Although many gather at church on Saturdays, Sundays or other days of worship, their hearts are not with God. They only focus on what they can get from Him. Some hearts and minds are on their way to make illicit gains and worldly acts. They choose not to focus on what God is saying to them.

The Israelites sat with the prophet, pretending to be interested in the truth of God. All the while, their minds were on unjust gains. With their mouths, they claimed they wanted the ways of God, but their hearts were far from Him. Today, let us not make the same careless mistake. Instead, may we listen to the voice of God through His servants. Let us willingly follow His instruction. To listen to and follow God's instruction is the pathway of life.

Day 34

"Indeed to them you are nothing more than one who sings love songs with a beautiful voice and plays an instrument well, for they hear your words but do not put them into practice. When all this comes true and it surely will, then they will know that a prophet has been among them."

Eze 33:32-33

They Will Only Realize When It Is Too Late

God knew the hearts of the Israelites. Although they claimed they wanted to know what He had to say through His prophet, He knew that they did not mean it. Many Israelites did not heed the call to repentance. They thought the prophet was a joke, only mocking what He said.

Oh, so sad it is right now that many who read the word of God and listen to the preacher, take God and His messengers for a joke! These devotionals are from God, speaking to people to repent and live right. Do not take God, His church, His prophets, or His messengers for a joke. If you do, you may well be joking your way to hellfire. Repent sincerely and serve the Lord. Search for those who have not received Jesus Christ as Lord and Saviour. Christians, let us stay the course and never look back.

The coming of The Lord God Almighty is near. Each day the signs are all over the place. Noah warned for many years, yet they took him for a joke. Only his family believed and was safe in the ark. Subsequently, the entire world was drowned, saving only Noah and those who believed. The unbelief of the people did not postpone God visiting with the judgement of a mighty flood of a disproportionate level.

Today, the message is similar. People must turn from their wickedness to God.

If you are not a Christian and are reading this message, you have heard. He who has ears to hear, let him hear what the Sovereign Spirit of God is saying right now. He says repent and turn to Him immediately before it is too late. Do not wait until mercy is gone.

Do not wait until, after hearing all this time, you just realise that it is all too late.

Day 35

The word of The Lord came unto me, saying, "Son of man, prophesy against the shepherds of Israel, prophesy and say unto them, Thus saith The Lord God unto the shepherds; woe be to the shepherds of Israel that do feed themselves! Should not the shepherds feed the flocks? Ye eat the fat, and you clothe yourselves with the wool, ye kill them that are fed: but ye feed not the flock."

Eze 34:1-3

Greedy Leaders, Be Careful!

So many leaders in different spheres of life have perfected the art of becoming fat at their subjects' expense. Greed has characterised the life of so many leaders. They have no time to care for their flocks, merely stuffing their pockets and bellies.

Those greedy and selfish leaders of Israel had only one agenda: to be rich by any means possible. They did not care who got hurt or died, so long as their craving desires were satisfied. So sad was the plight of their poverty-stricken subjects, but to the leaders that was alright. They had no heart for their suffering subjects. Oh, what a tragedy!

Today, it is no different. Many leaders have no time for their subjects. They are just busy fattening their pockets. They rob the poor and kill just to fill their bank accounts. Their disgusting appetites must be satisfied.

The church today has not escaped from some of these greedy people. They must become rich at the expense of their congregants, and it must happen at any cost. Some want an extremely lavish lifestyle. Having a private jet, a large mansion, an extravagant bank account and the most expensive car at poor members' expense is just the norm. Do they even care if some of their members have dinner? That is not their business! Their business is to swindle these poor people and make themselves rich. Sad!

You greedy leaders, what will you tell God? You rob people to become rich, but will you enjoy your gain? Don't you know that ill-gotten gain will fast disappear? Repent and give back that which you have swindled from the poor. Your church members and God will forgive you, and you will thus escape His wrath.

Day 36

They (sheep) were scattered, because there is no Shepherd: and they became meat to all the beasts of the field, when they were scattered. My sheep wandered through all the mountains, and upon every high hill: yea, my flock was scattered upon the face of the Earth and none did seek to search after them.

Eze 34:5-6

The Flocks Have Gone Astray

Jesus placed heavy emphasis on taking care of His flock. To Him, each of His sheep is the apple of His eye. He does not want anyone to mess around with those who are His. Thus, He carefully handpicked and equipped those who should lead His flock.

Pastoring God's flock is a serious job. No one should assume the pastorate unless God has called and done the ordination. While it is good to aspire to do great things for Almighty God, one should only venture as He leads. One does not want to mess with or mess up any of His children! As a result, He does not expect the shepherds to disadvantage any of the sheep. He will act, lest any member of the flock is led astray by the one He places in charge. Oh, if anyone should cause any of His sheep to go astray, it would be to one's detriment. In St Luke 17:2, He warned,

> "It were better for him that a millstone were hanged about his neck, and he cast into the sea, than that he should offend one of these little ones."

That is the value He places on His sheep.

In Ezekiel's time, those in charge of God's flock did not express care and love toward the sheep. Their desires were far from what God wanted for them. Self-centeredness was the order of their lives. Due to their passion for illicit living and delving in greed for money, they allowed God's flock to be scattered. The flock not only scattered far and wide, but they were also devoured by heartless wolves. Oh, beloved, that was a serious problem to God Almighty. Not just one sheep from the fold was lost — they were all scattered, all over the place.

Jesus' attitude towards leading and caring for His sheep was spot on. Whenever one of them went astray, He made every effort to find that lost sheep. Oh, what care, reconciliation, forgiveness, and kindness revealed through His love! In St Matt 18:12-13, Jesus tickled the minds of His hearers in the following words:

> "How think ye? If a man have an hundred sheep, and one of them be gone astray, doth he not leave the ninety and nine, and goeth into the mountains, and seeketh that which is gone? If so be that he find it, verily I say unto you, he rejoiceth more of that sheep, than of the ninety and nine which went not astray."

What love on full display! It is Jesus' style of leadership that must be the example of all our shepherds.

Shepherds, although the work is not easy, trust God to keep you through. There are many sheep who have already gone astray, and some are on the brink of going away from the sheepfold. Therefore, let us do our best by going all the way for them.

Some shepherds are judgemental in their approach toward fallen members. They behave as if such members are irredeemable, so they employ measures to keep down the already dispirited and wounded. This is truly a self-righteous stance. Did Christ give you the permission to cast one who is wounded to the back of the church to suffer more embarrassment and indignation? Did Jesus give you the permission to suspend one from your congregation? Who gave you the authority to expel one from your congregation and subsequently from the Body of Christ? Where have you sent him or her? Truly, to Satan and Hell! Why not express a little more patience? If some of those who claimed to have known Christ employed the strategy of reconciliation, forgiveness, and love, some of our churches would be in a better place.

Jesus Christ was a friend to the hopeless. Yes, He was a friend to the marginalised. He worked to bring back the strayed. Oh, for self-righteous shepherds to employ His strategy and stop behaving as if they are gods over their congregations!

Friends, let us take care of those who are in the flock. Let us do our best to win those who have strayed. If we try in accordance with what Jesus desires and they refuse, then we would have done our part, and Christ would be glorified. Peace.

Day 37

"I will feed them in a good pasture, and upon the high mountains of Israel shall their fold be: there shall they lie in a good fold, and in a fat pasture shall they feed upon the mountains of Israel. I will feed My flock, and I will cause them to lie down," saith The Lord.

Eze 34:14-15

Jehovah Jireh, My Great Provider

From the beginning of mankind to the present, the Lord God Almighty has provided for His crowning glory. No human is void of God's provision, especially if they have committed themselves to serve Him.

God watches over His flock, and each member of His fold is as special and equal as the other. To Him, none is more important than the other. Consequently, He will not provide for some and disregard the needs of others.

He watched His flock for years and took note of how the earthly shepherds robbed, maimed, and disadvantaged them. He had to act against those unscrupulous shepherds as well as to rescue His precious flock.

Oh, beloved, God Almighty fed His flock in the very best pastureland. He gave them the best. They had it all to their comfort. He ensured that His flock was properly secured, safe from the enemy. He made sure those bad shepherds could never again reign in terror over them.

Truth is, no one can do more than his or her allotted time. The unscrupulous shepherds of Israel may have felt they could take advantage of the flock whenever and wherever they wanted. Yet God said of them, "Your time is up."

God had to remove those corrupt leaders to bless His people. He will surely perform the same feat again. Oh, yes friends: At times when God is about to lavish His provision upon His people, He will remove some of the stumbling blocks out of the way. Those shepherds who practised thievery and made themselves fat at the expense of God's flock had to receive due punishment from God Himself. Let us keep in mind beloved that some governments, departments, businesses, offices, schools, churches, and other organizations will never prosper under their leadership if corruption is the order of the day. When the leadership has no care and regard toward the people being led and when little or no accountability is exhibited, something is drastically wrong. Furthermore, when partiality reigns supreme, that type of leadership is highly negative. God will bring it to an end. Such a rule or leadership may seem long but will not be forever. Negative leadership only breeds negative vibes in the organization and consequently little or no production is realised.

God was Israel's Jehovah Jireh. He provided the best pastureland for them. He ensured that all their needs were met. But most of all, He made His presence felt amongst them. Oh, what a wonderful God who takes care of His beloved flock. Just as how He provided for Israel, He is providing for you and me. Is He your Jehovah Jireh? Yes, He is! Oh yes, He is, and the truth is, He will go all the way to bless you. He will remove corrupt leaders who have been a blockade to your prosperity and progress. Jehovah Jireh, our Provider.

Day 38

"I will make them and the places round about My hill a blessing; and I will cause the shower to come down in his season; there shall be showers of blessing. The tree of the field shall yield her fruit, and the Earth shall yield her increase, and they shall be safe in their land, and shall know that I Am The Lord, when I have broken the bands of their yoke, and delivered them out of the hand of those that served themselves of them."

Eze 34:26-27

Showers of Blessing

Have you ever longed for a shower of blessing? Your season may have been dry for a long time. Almost everything you do seems to be failing. Not to mention, those past blessings that you once treasured are also taken from you. But something is about to change. It is time for the showers we need.

The saddened, sick, outcast, destitute Israelites had reached suffering at unprecedented levels. Their suffering was mainly because of their evil shepherds, who ensured their lives were in the worst, most miserable state.

Almighty God, however, saw their plight and came to their rescue. He not only rescued them — He also re-established a covenant of peace with them. One condition of the covenant was for God to bring showers of blessing upon His people. God brought back His children to safety and poured upon them showers of blessing. The Israelites felt God's blessing upon them in an unmeasured fashion. God gave them double for their trouble.

My friend, you have experienced real hardship, but the time for the showers of blessing from God is coming. The sound of abundance of rain can be heard — if you listen.

D. W. Whittle (1883) pencilled the beautiful hymn entitled, 'There shall be showers of blessing.' Let us sing along.

There shall be showers of blessing:
 This is the promise of love;
There shall be seasons refreshing,
 Sent from the Saviour above.

Showers of blessing,
 Showers of blessing we need;
Mercy-drops round us are falling,
 But for the showers we plead.

There shall be showers of blessing—
 Precious reviving again;
Over the hills and the valleys,
 Sound of abundance of rain.

There shall be showers of blessing;
 Send them upon us, O Lord!
Grant to us now a refreshing;
 Come, and now honour Thy Word.

There shall be showers of blessing;
 O that today they might fall,
Now as to God we're confessing,
 Now as on Jesus we call!

There shall be showers of blessing,
 If we but trust and obey;

There shall be seasons refreshing,
If we let God have His way.

You have suffered greatly, but now the Lord showers you with His wonderful blessing. Receive it all in Jesus' name. It is your time of reaping, renewal and refreshing, so rejoice.

Day 39

"Then they will know that I, The Lord their God, Am with them and that they, the House of Israel, are My people, declares The Sovereign Lord. You My sheep, the sheep of My pasture, are people, and I Am your God, declares The Sovereign Lord."

Eze 34:30-31

I Am a Child of God

God's love for His Israelite children was not only demonstrated through actions but also by His declarations. God told His people that they were His, and He theirs. God had to speak the word to them since, although they were being blessed by Him, many did not know His voice. God wanted them to know that He was their Father and Friend.

A declaration has great weight. It reveals ownership and comforts the hearts of the hearers. To hear the King of Kings make a declaration over one's life was of special mention. Not only did the declaration signify ownership or bring comfort — but it also signalled to the enemies around to back off.

To be aligned with a particular individual can either bring special favour or curses. However, when God declares someone to be His, favour is the order upon that individual's life. Being favoured by God suggests a high level of grace and protection. When one is protected by God, it will cause the enemy to think deep as to how to attack. The enemy will not only be afraid of the protected but also the Protector. Thus, he will walk wide and say, "That one is protected so do not go near him or her."

Once God declares you to be His, you will never come second — if you put God first. He will take up for you and defend you since you are one hundred per cent His.

Today, God declares that you are His child. Do you believe His declaration? If you really believe, then act positively. Stop the puny behaviour. Stop believing the lies of the Devil. Remember, the word of Jesus Christ cannot lie. All we must do is to believe what He said. Have you heard his voice?

> You are healed! You are rich! I Am with you! I Am protecting you! I will see you through! I will supply all your needs!

Listen, people of God! For Almighty God to declare that you are His, means He has taken sole authority over your life. He is responsible for you. Believe Him because the declaration is legitimate. The declaration is authentic. The declaration is clear. The declaration is decisive. The declaration is bold, and the declaration is final. You belong to Almighty God. *Shalom.*

Day 40

The word of The Lord came to me: "Son of man, set your face against Mount Seir, prophesy against it and say: This is what The Sovereign Lord says: I Am against you, Mount Seir, and I will stretch out My hand against you and make you a desolate waste. You have said, 'These two nations and countries will be ours and we will take possession of them,' even though I The Lord was there."

Eze 35:1-3 & 10.

Leave the Man's Wife Alone!

Mount Seir was a mountainous region between the Dead Sea and the Gulf of Aqaba, running along the South-eastern border with Judah. That area is presently occupied by Syria. The original people of Mount Seir were called the Horites. Their land was invaded, and its descendants were destroyed by the descendants of Esau, who then occupied the land. Those occupiers called themselves Seirites or Edomites.

Israel was descended from Jacob whose twin brother was Esau. The Edomites were therefore closely related to Israel by blood. Although closely related, however, they were extremely far apart. Today they are still separated by distance.

During Israel's time of turmoil, the people of Mount Seir made the destructive decision to further ravage their blood relatives. God was not amused. They decided to invade the already broken-down Israel and Judah, with the intention of violating what was left.

It was clear that although Israel and Judah were God's estranged wives, He was still in the picture. He revealed, "though I the Lord was there," Mount Seir decided to take possession. Ah, beloved, it is a danger to trespass on God's property, mainly His wife.

God decided to destroy Edom and Mount Seir. They were violent towards Israel and they were inimical toward their neighbour. They rejoiced over Judah's downfall, invaded their land in times of distress, and they took Israel's land and ensured the death of her citizens. God was present when all these unfortunate things happened to His wives. He was watching all the time. Although His spouse had disrespected Him, He was still married; there was no divorce involved. How could Mount Seir and Edom feel the opportunity was right to take over the wives of Another? Serious!

It is not spiritually or morally correct for anyone to take another's wife simply because that wife is experiencing marital issues with her husband. To absorb another's spouse is adultery. It is a clear violation of God's holy stance and His laws. No one who is against God's tenets and laws can win. It does not matter how important one thinks he or she is. If one is intimately involved with another's spouse, that is a suicidal act of the soul.

Mount Seir and Edom used violence against Israel and entered her land illegally to take possession. The country found itself in trouble with God. It will be the same with the man or woman who unlawfully enters another's marriage and takes over another's partner. It does not matter if that new relationship blossomed into another marriage. God will act. There are laws that God has put in place. If violated, there is a consequence that must be paid.

Beloved, marriage is honourable whenever God sanctions it. Today, I plead with anyone whose ambition is to unlawfully enter a marriage. Do not go there. It is a death trap. To those who have already broken another person's marriage, you need to get out of the people's life. Repent of your wickedness and turn to Jesus Christ who will abundantly forgive you and receive you as His child. Run, run, run, run from adultery. It is a trap set and a gateway to Hell.

Day 41

"You rejoiced when the inheritance of the House of Israel became desolate, that is how I will treat you. You will be desolate, O Mount Seir, you and all of Edom. Then they will know that I Am The Lord."

Eze 35:15

He Who Laughs Last, Laughs Best

Oh, the Edomites rejoiced at the calamity that their neighbour and blood relative Israel suffered. They laughed and were ecstatic with thoughts of entering their neighbour's property. But they might not have known the phrase, "Those who laugh last, laugh best." God laughed at their ecstasy and foolishness.

God has a way of laughing at fools who make fun of His children. In Psalm 59:8, David recited, "You, O Lord, laugh at them; You scoff at all those nations." Also, in Psalm 2:1, David sought the Lord concerning some boastful persons. "Why do the nations conspire, and the peoples plot in vain?" He, however, posited God's response to his rhetorical question. Regarding the plotters in verses 4-6, he writes,

> "The One enthroned in Heaven laughs; the Lord scoffs at them. Then He rebuked them in His anger and terrifies them in His wrath saying, I have installed My King on Zion My Holy Hill."

Ah, beloved, whenever God laughs and scoffs at those who trouble and laugh at His children, those troublemakers are in serious problems.

Dearly beloved, they laughed at you while you were down. Some even took advantage of you and your situation. But try and push through. The joke will not be on you forever. For a child of God, the Lord is both defence and offence. Don't you trouble 'Zion.' O, yes, don't ever mess with 'Zion!' God will laugh and scoff at you if you mess with His child.

Day 42

"Son of man, prophesy to the mountains of Israel and say, O mountains of Israel, hear the word of The Lord. This is what The Sovereign Lord says: The enemy said of you, "Aha! The ancient heights have become our possession." This is what The Sovereign Lord says: In My burning zeal I have spoken against the rest of the nations, and against Edom, for with glee and with malice in their hearts they made My land their own possession so that they might plunder its pastureland."

Eze 36:1-2 & 5

The Gang Is Destroyed

The nations around Israel ganged up against her. The already battered Israel was about to experience more ridicule from those who hated her. An already scorned nation was about to face more wrath from her neighbours who wanted blood. The nations' conspiracy against God's people was at an all-time high and they were about to enter for the kill. Israel's neighbour thought the opportunity was spot on for them to take over an already ravaged people. But little did they know, Israel had a defence, the Great Counsellor of Counsels.

Have you ever been conspired against and ganged upon by people? Have persons surrounded you to harm you, because of your righteous stance? Do not be surprised. Just remember that during these times, God will still defend you.

I have been to that place. Because I stood up for the right principles, people swarmed me like ants. They tried to evict me from what God had provided for me. I was once told by an official, "When I go to Rome, I should do as the Romans do." I thought that such a statement was irrelevant for me — I would never join a gang operating in immoral activities. If your stance is for righteousness, God will defend you against those who gang up against you.

Some time ago, I was involved in a matter in another jurisdiction. A young defendant pled guilty to an offence before the court. According to him, he pled guilty on the advice of his lawyer. Whilst in a conversation with his counsel, the lawyer questioned, *what would be his client's defence if he had not pled guilty?* The lawyer was supposed to be his defence. At a time when he was down, the defendant needed a quality defence to assist him. What he said did not add up.

Though down, the Israelites were not completely out. They had the Quality Defence — God Almighty. He came to their rescue. God would never sit down and allow for the entire nation of Israel to be completely destroyed by her enemies. He had to act, and He Himself destroyed the gang that came up against her.

Have you ever felt as if everything and everyone is against you? You may feel as if you are down and out and O, it appears that everything you do and try is just a total failure. You even cry out to God and it seems He is far away from you. It appeared as if He stopped answering your prayers. What is worse, your enemies have been at it against you. It seems as if they were winning — and you are losing. O, what a difficult and indifferent time you have experienced!

At what you consider to be your last, God will stand up for you. He is your defence. He will never allow your enemies to triumph over you. Yes, you think it is the last, but God is standing up for you. When the Devil says 'No,' Jesus says 'Yes.'

When the Devil laughs and tells you, "You have no defence," Jesus says, "I Am your Defender."

Today, beloved, God will show up in your lowest moment. Believe Him. He came through for Israel. You bet He will come through for you. *Shalom*, my friend. It is not over.

Day 43

"Therefore prophesy concerning the land of Israel and say to the mountains and hills, to the ravines and valleys: This is what The Sovereign Lord says: I speak in My jealous wrath because you have suffered the scorn of the nations. You O mountains of Israel, will produce branches and fruit for My people Israel, for they will soon come home. I Am concerned for you and will look on you with favour; you will be ploughed and sworn, and I will multiply the number of people upon you, even the whole House of Israel. The towns will be inhabited and the ruins rebuilt. I will increase the number of men and animals upon you, and they will be fruitful and become numerous. I will settle people on you as in the past and make you prosper more than before. Then you will know that I Am The Lord."

Eze 36:6, 8-12

From Scorn to Approval

God's children had undergone severe disgrace. Little life was left amongst them. However, God had a plan. In His plan, He revisited the remnants. He decided that they had had enough trouble and so for their misfortune, He blessed them.

The Israelites were scorned, but from scorn, they arose to approval. Yes, beloved, they were lifted from derision to praise. They were mocked, but God exalted them from mockery to favour and respect. They who were once ridiculed, have now risen to a life of pleasure. O, the people of utter disdain had now become the delight of those around them. It was God who took them from the low and lifted them to the high. He caused the barren to become fruitful, so Israel once more became populated.

Dearly beloved, you have been demoted by man, and they have poured scorn upon you. They made it their way to disgrace and scandalise you. But God is about to lift you up out of your lowliness and set you on high. Yes, friend, you are the apple of His eyes.

Day 44

"I will cause people, My people Israel, to walk upon you. They will possess you, and you will be their inheritance; you will never again deprive them of their children."

Eze 36:12.

Poverty to Prosperity

The Government of Jamaica has a slogan that they currently use — "Poverty to Prosperity." However, most Jamaicans do not have a clue as to what prosperity they are speaking about. Today, poverty, low wages and lack constitute many Jamaican families who continue to suffer. The irony of the matter is that the riches of this nation remains within the hands of ten per cent of the people, while the majority grope around living from paycheck to paycheck or charity.

In general, we fail to recognise the evil practised by some in leadership positions. Corruption easily continues to thrive in very high places in this nation. If we are speaking of prosperity, let us include all Jamaicans, and not just a few being the hefty beneficiaries. Jamaica will never be prosperous under the current situation of thievery, corruption, greed, and scandal. The hearts of our people, from leadership to the common man, need to be transformed from greed and sin to righteousness through the blood of Jesus Christ.

The Israelites almost lost everything. Those who remained became stricken in poverty. They were so poor that one's neighbour was not positioned to assist the hungry and weak. In their distress, they may have had time to reminisce about Jehovah. He led their ancestors through the wilderness. He provided manna and quail for eating purposes. He gave them a cloud to cover more than two million people from the hot sun. He provided light that was as bright as light produced from nuclear energy to guide them during the night-time. He gave them the best fresh drinking water from the rock to quench their thirst. God richly provided for the nearly two and a half million people of Israel as they wandered through the desert. The remnant knew of His great provision. Since God did that for their ancestors, they believed He would do something special for them and surely, He did. He would not abandon His children to be ravaged by their neighbours.

Almighty God told the Israelites that He would move them from poverty to prosperity. The poverty-stricken were unable to afford basic amenities, but in one moment, God changed it all for His children. In God's Book of Provision, all are included. He does not favour some and leave others for dead. People from all strata of life were effectively cared for by Almighty God, and all became prosperous. The land became once more productive, and instead of anguish and pain, there was a noise of jubilation.

When a nation becomes prosperous, its people will walk in safety. There will be no need to fear leaders and those who swore to protect and serve. Jobs will be available — not superficial ones, but good jobs for its citizens. Children will be able to grow without the worry of being robbed of their innocence. The old will be lavished with respect. Great will be the economy of that nation. Surely it will be the envy of the world!

Jamaica can move from poverty to prosperity. May we as a people learn to respect each other, be honest, surrender all our lives to Almighty God and faithfully serve Him. My fellow Jamaican brothers and sisters, may we repent of our sins and live for God. In this way, the blessings of Jesus Christ in all their fullness will rest upon Jamaica, land we love. *Shalom.*

Day 45

"This is what The Sovereign Lord says: because people say to you, 'You devour men and deprive your nation of its children,' therefore you will no longer devour men or make your nation childless, declares The Sovereign Lord. No longer will I make you hear the taunts of the nations, and no longer will you suffer the scorn of the peoples or cause your nation to fall, declares The Sovereign Lord."

Eze 36:13-15

Ignore the Negative Talks Levelled Against You

The Lord has a way of allowing you to become a selective listener. Not everything said of you, you should hear. Some of what is said of you may bring you grief and pain, so it is best not to hear everything said. If you were to hear the unkind things that some people have said about you, maybe you would faint.

People can be so cruel. They often do not care what they say about another person — so long as their evil intentions and desires are satisfied. They do not care who they hurt with their viperous tongues, babbling against their brothers and sisters. The Sovereign Lord will not have His children hear everything said of them, as the pain from hearing negatives may cause a lifetime of grief and unforgiveness.

Israel's covetous neighbours had so much fun speaking evil of her. Their desire was to possess Israel's land and her inheritance at any cost. They tried to gain leverage above Israel by using their tongues to taunt a people already battered. Their hatred was expressed in what they said of her. They had nothing good to say of Israel, and God knew that if His children were to hear all the unkind remarks levelled against them, they would have become despondent and fearful. As a result, God did not allow them to hear all the taunts levelled against them. He allowed them to employ the strategy of selective listening.

It is not always wise to hear everything said about you. What one hears can shape the way he or she behaves. It is easy to listen to negative people. What they say can have a profound effect on one's life. Be careful whom you associate yourself with, as many do not mean you any good. Furthermore, some will use their enticing lips to entrap one into sin. Stay away from negative people. It is impossible for a negative person not to divulge negative information from his or her tongue. Negative words breed negative actions, and negative actions produce negative results.

Today, your enemies may be taunting you with their lies and negative talks. Do not pay them any attention. Continue to dwell in the secret place of the Most High. There, you will listen to God's voice while shutting out the voice of your taunters.

Forget those negatives that were levelled against you. What they have said does not characterise your life. Develop the attitude of selective listening as it is not everything said of you is geared for your growth and development — certain things spoken to you are meant to destroy you. Consequently, ask the Lord to guide you in what and who you listen to.

Day 46

"Son of man, when the people of Israel were living in their own land, they defiled it by their own conduct and their actions. Their conduct was like a woman's monthly uncleanness in My sight. So I poured out My wrath on them because they had shed blood in the land and because they had defiled it with their idols. I dispersed them among the nations, and they were scattered through the countries; I judged them according to their conduct and their actions. Wherever they went among the nations they profaned My Holy Name, for it was said of them, 'These are the Lord's people, and yet they had to leave His land.' I had concern for My Holy Name, which the House of Israel profaned among the nations where they had gone."

Eze 36:17-21

You Are an Ambassador — Represent Well

The Israelites were given the land of Canaan by Almighty God to enjoy its benefits. They were, however, informed by God that they were not to worship any other gods. Worshipping false gods would be a serious problem between themselves and God. God does not tolerate idolatry and furthermore, He does not share His glory.

He expected His people to worship Him in spirit and in truth, to represent Him to the nations around them. They were to be His ambassadors to their neighbours. However, they failed to live up to what God called them to. Consequently, they were driven away from the land they were given. Yet still, wherever they were scattered, they still did not represent God.

Hundreds of years later, the Church in Jerusalem was being persecuted. Christians were scattered to different parts of the

Earth. Those Christians, however, in their banishment status represented Christ in the foreign jurisdictions they entered. Luke gave a vivid account of their ambassadorial duties in Acts 11:19-21,

> "Now those who had been scattered by the persecution that broke out when Stephen was killed travelled as far as Phoenicia, Cyprus, and Antioch, spreading the word only among Jews. Some of them, however, men from Cyprus and Cyrene went to Antioch and began to speak to Greeks also, telling them the Good News about The Lord Jesus. The Lord's hand was with them, and a great number of people believed and turn to The Lord."

During Ezekiel's time, God scattered the Israelites amongst the nations, because of their disdainful lifestyle. Yet they did not repent and represent Almighty God. Unlike them, the Church of Jerusalem was scattered through persecution and they spread the Good News of Jesus Christ to foreigners. Wherever we are, we should represent Jesus Christ and do it well. We are His ambassadors.

Those Israelites who were scattered by God could not represent Him, since their lifestyle was not in accordance with the principles of God. However, we can be true ambassadors of God. We must submit ourselves to His leadership and guidance. God is depending on us to represent Him well.

Each day, we are expected to be a living example of Jesus Christ to the world. We are expected to live as Jesus did. Too often, many say they are Christians, but their lifestyle depicts something else. The world must see Jesus in us. We are not here for the praises of men, but to honour God Almighty. Let

Day 47

"I had concern for My Holy Name, which the House of Israel profaned among the nations where they had gone."

Eze 36:21

The Lord's Holy Name

It is a dangerous thing to misuse the Lord's name. Taking the Lord's name in vain or using His name to commit an infraction or evil, amounts up to blasphemy. The name of the Lord is extremely holy, as it is His name that speaks about His character. In Exodus 20:7, God warned the Israelites, "Thou shalt not take the name of the Lord thy God in vain; for the Lord will not hold him guiltless that takes His name in vain." God was so concerned about the misuse of His name by the Israelites. They disrespected Him with their lives, yet they kept saying they belonged to Him.

God prohibits anyone from using His name in vain. If we are hypocritical in our living, making a profession of His name but not living for Him, we are taking His name in vain. Beloved, Israel broke the covenant made between them and God. In this, they took His name in vain. If we break the promise we made with God and refuse to perform the vows we made with Him, that too is taking His name in vain.

There are people who rashly swear by the name of the Lord by taking an oath or by false swearing. Those persons are dangerously poised against Him. Beloved, that is taking His name in vain. Many often use the Lord's name carelessly, loosely, or lightly; but such activities are profanity against God.

God has a right to be concerned about His name when it is blasphemed, and He will certainly act. It is great profanity to claim that one is a servant of God when his or her heart is filled with hatred against one's co-workers. How can anyone claim to love God, yet hate her mother-in-law with all her guts? How can you claim to be a pastor, leading the church, yet you treat your wife with great disdain? If you do, you are a hypocrite, and your prayers are not answered by God. Is money the most important element of your message? Do you treat people as things and not humans? How can anyone preach the word of God, yet live in fornication? To live in any sexual sin is a clear slap in the face of Almighty God. God hates sin, and He warns us to stay away from not only sin but its very appearance.

It is virtually impossible to serve God and at the same time take the Lord's name in vain. If you are living in unforgiveness, do not pretend to be serving God when you refuse to forgive your sister or brother. It is an indictment on anyone to take the Lord's name in vain. If you do, God will not hold you guiltless.

Israel profaned the name of the Lord amongst the nations. They pretended to be servants of The Most High God. Yet, at the same time, they were bowing down to idols. Their intentions were against Almighty God, yet they wanted all the blessings He could give them. God was concerned about His name that was profaned, and He acted.

Beloved, it is a dangerous sin to take the name of the Lord in vain. If you are a Christian, then live for Jesus. However, if you are hiding behind a mask, doing whatever you please and claiming to be a child of God, you are taking His name in vain. Those who take His name in vain will be dealt with. Be warned: The name of the Lord is holy. Do not take it in vain.

Day 48

"Therefore say to the House of Israel, This is what The Sovereign Lord says: It is not for your sake, O House of Israel, that I Am going to do these things, but for the sake of My Holy Name, which you have profaned among the nations where you have gone. I will show the holiness of My Great Name, which has been profaned among the nations, the Name you have profaned among them. Then the nations will know that I Am The Lord, declares The Sovereign Lord, when I show myself holy through you before their eyes."

Eze 36:22-23

For the Glory of My Holy Name

Almighty God is changeless and perfect in all His ways. His character cannot be improved upon. He remains the same as He was, ten thousand years ago. He is forever true and will remain that way. There is just one character that He honours above His name — His Word. The Psalmist incredibly revealed in Ps. 138:2, "God has magnified His Word above all His Name." What God has done is to declare that He stands by His Word, as He Himself is the Living Word. Thus, His Name which bears His character comes next. His Glorious Name is holy, and no one should profane His matchless name.

God made a covenant with the people of Israel. That agreement was to last for all time. The covenant was binding on the parties, and all were expected to do their part. Israel, however, did not honour the agreement and thus paid the price.

In their dishonouring of Almighty God, they profaned His Glorious Name. Still, God had to protect His legacy, His Glorious Name. That is what He did.

God's move to honour His Holy Name among the nations was unprecedented. The people He covenanted with did not showcase His Holy Name to the nations. Therefore, He had to do it Himself. God let the nations know His Mighty, Holy Name by what He did. He demonstrated to Israel's neighbours that He was God as He overthrew those nations.

God also allowed His Holy Name to be on display. He showed Himself holy through the same people who profaned His Holy Name. He gave them a chance to show forth His glory. But why did God do it? Many long years before the nation of Israel was established, God made a covenant with their forefather Abraham. Abraham was faithful to God, and God decided that He would honour the covenant, irrespective of what those Israelites had done. That was His way of staying in the agreement. He is a covenant-keeping God.

Dearly beloved, let us make ourselves available to God, so He can manifest Himself through us to those around us. Yes, friends, He has covenanted with us. Indeed, we added our signatures to the eternal document when we accepted Jesus Christ as Lord and Saviour. Through the binding agreement with us, He promises to showcase His Holy Name. His Name bears His character. It must be seen in us since we are covenant partners with Him. O yes, for the glory of His Name, He will highlight His character through you and me. *Shalom.*

Day 49

"For I will take you out of the nations; I will gather you from all the countries and bring you back into your own land."

I Will Bring You Home

The wise man King Solomon understood the Sovereign Lord rescues people by His powerful Name. Watch this! In Proverbs 18:10 he revealed, "The Name of The Lord is a strong tower; the righteous run to it and are safe." God's name was now a banner for His children hovering over their heads. God made a bold statement: "I come to rescue My children."

Jehovah-Nissi!

Yes, the Lord was Israel's banner, acting on their behalf with a great rescue mission. God's presence was highly demonstrated by His Name. His power was well executed under the auspices of His Magnificent Name, Jehovah. Oh, the presence and power of Almighty God were the banner under which the Israelites were rescued. What a Name! That Mighty Name, Jehovah that rescued the Israelites from amongst the nations.

Today, The Great Name of Jesus Christ is our banner. He continues the rescue mission. No one can experience eternal salvation except by the Name of Jesus Christ. It is by the Name of Jesus Christ that humans are saved. God wants to rescue people from their sins. He wants to be a banner for them and give them an eternal home as their inheritance. Sin, however, is a serious deterrent. It has caused mankind to be separated from God.

Too many are deceived, believing that there are several avenues to eternal life and Heaven. Oh, no! No man, woman, boy, or girl can be saved except by the Great Name of Jesus Christ. It is above all names. The name Selassie has never saved anyone and still has no power to effect salvation. The name Mohammed has never produced salvation and it remains powerless as it was since 620 AD. Confucius, the Virgin Mary, Shiva, Krishna, Vishnu, Ganesha, Rama, Hanuman, Lakshmi, Durga, Kali, Saraswati, Brahma, and Guru Nanak never gave anyone salvation. Clearly, they and their names are dead and remain powerless.

The Great Name of Jesus is a strong tower. It is being advertised to the world, offering salvation to all. Children of God, let us echo the Name of Jesus Christ, expressing it loudly and clearly. Let us inform the world that salvation is found in no one else but in Jesus. May we be carriers of this great news, the Gospel. Souls are dying and going to the pit of Hell. The trip is unforgettable and a no-return one. Let us win the lost at any cost.

Advertise Jesus Christ, my brothers and sisters! Do not apologize to anyone for proclaiming the Great Name of Jesus!

Day 50

"I will sprinkle clean water on you, and you will be clean; I will cleanse you from all your impurities and from all your idols. I will give you a new heart and put a new spirit in you; I will remove from you your heart of stone and give you a heart of flesh."

Eze 36:25-26

Relationship Demands Pureness

For God to enjoy a wholesome relationship with His people, the need to be pure was an absolute must. The Israelites were steadfast in their sins, worshipping idols and making God angry. God, however, hatched a plan to bring them back to Himself, and certainly, He did.

Almighty God longed for a relationship with His estranged wife Israel. He put forward the initiative to regain that longing fellowship. He approached them with words of love, care, and romance. He forgave their adulterous lifestyle. Oh yes, beloved, He called them back to Himself, washed them with clean water, and made them pure.

He gave them a new heart of love. The old stubborn, stony heart was replaced with a heart of flesh. Israel experienced new feelings for her Husband, Almighty God. The relationship was in full swing. In Ezekiel's time, a love like that was nowhere else to be found. The Lover and His wife dwelt in His secret place in total commitment.

Today, Jesus Christ longs for fellowship with those estranged from Him. He proposes to give a new heart of flesh filled with love. Oh, yes, He wants to replace that stony heart with a heart of love.

So many have been living in a backslidden state and have fallen out of love with Almighty God. To all those who have lost their first love for God, He calls out to you and say: "I love you and want to have fellowship with you. Will you accept My invitation?" If you accept the invitation Jesus Christ is giving you, He will wash you in His blood. He will robe you in garments of white with a loving embrace. You see, friends, Jesus will do the washing with His blood, as it is the blood that purifies from sins. After purification, He will take you to His secret place for intimacy, where secrets are revealed.

Today, so many are members of the church, yet they experience no real relationship with Jesus Christ. They have been experiencing dryness and no intimacy. Oh, how long some have not heard the voice of God whispering in their ears or speaking to their hearts! Do you want to know the secrets of the Saviour's heart? Do you want to hear His precious voice? If so, then get to His secret place. If you get close to the King, you will see and know things many are not privy to.

Brothers and sisters, may we seek to get closer and closer to the Lord. Oh, the closer one gets, the more one will know and see the glory of the intimate Lord. Relationship of the highest order will be realised. Intimacy, intimacy, intimacy is the call. Come to intimacy!

Day 51

"I will put My Spirit in you and move you to follow My decrees and be careful to keep My laws. You will live in the land I gave your forefathers; you will be My people, and I will be your God."

Eze 36:27-28

The Eternal Bond

Almighty God purposed to put His Sweet Holy Spirit in His once estranged wife. He proposed to form an eternal bond between them. It was God the Husbandman who was going to place Himself in His wife Israel. The Holy Spirit would act as the connecting agent, thus reproducing life within her.

A most wonderful story unfolds in Genesis 2:7: "The Lord God formed the man from the dust of the ground and breathed into his nostrils the Breath of Life, and the man became a living being." O, what a wonderful story! Almighty God moulded man's body from the Earth. Whilst lying on the ground, man was dead. God, however, breathed the Breath of Life — His Spirit — into the dead body, and in an instant, man became alive.

Man did not receive life because of an organized body, nor from what some teachers allude to as evolution. Instead, through God's direct intervention He placed Himself into man. The Breath of Life into man expresses a great life-giving principle. The body was formed from the dust yet dead. The Breath of Life, breathed by God, gave that same body life. This action paved the way for the very essence of Almighty God to reside in a man's body. Therefore, man is so connected to Almighty God: he receives life from the Breath of God, resulting in him bearing God's glorious image.

Man is so special to God since he is virtually part of Him and bears His image. Therefore, since the Breath of Life was placed into man, he is not an animal — contrary to what many teach. God did not breathe the Breath of Life into animals. Man is created in God's image, animals are not. Man is an eternal being and that is why after he dies, he goes to another world since he is a spiritual being. Animals are physical and when they die, they do not have a soul to face eternity.

The Greek word for Spirit is *pneuma*. This word means "to breathe" and it denotes the wind. Since the Spirit is characterised as the wind, one does not see the wind with the naked eyes but can feel its enormous power. It is the same when the Holy Spirit takes control of one's life. This individual is filled with God's power.

Israel belonged to God and to no one else. Note the possessive pronoun 'my' in our Scripture for reference. God said:

(1) "I will put 'My' Spirit in you"

(2) "to follow 'My' decrees"

(3) "and be careful to keep 'My' laws."

(4) "You will be 'My' people." God staked full ownership of Israel as His. They were His people to form an eternal bond through His precious Holy Spirit. His people were to follow His decrees and keep His laws. That reality sees God's people dwelling in a land of prosperity.

The same God Who imputed His Holy Spirit in Israel is with us today. Christians, God breathes His Holy Spirit in us. He gives us a guarantee that we are His and not another's. We must understand that we are possessively His and that we should therefore please Him in everything we think, speak, or do. Pleasing God comes at a cost. We may have to give up some people, career, assets, or other elements just to be His forever. The bonding process is serene. The Holy Spirit, as the Spirit of Peace, lives inside us. He conveys peace even amid the storm and helps us to please God. The believer bonded to Christ is filled with the love of the Father who owns him or her. Subsequently, it is virtually impossible for one who is filled with God's Spirit to hate another human or to live in a state of unforgiveness. Neither can the bonded live unseemingly.

The life of the bonded is to enjoy the good of the land. When the time for graduating from Earth becomes a reality, the Christian steps into eternity with Almighty God to enjoy its fullness.

Day 52

"I will save you from all your uncleanness. I will call for the corn and make it plentiful and will not bring famine upon you. I will increase the fruit of the trees and the crops of the field, so that you will no longer suffer disgrace among the nations because of famine.

Eze 36:29-30.

No More Crumbs

The days of lack and famine (dearth) had finally come to an end. Israel's God ensured that it would be a reality. Those who suffered from lack and scarcity were in the millions. Yes, the pains were real, especially when Israel's neighbours made fun of them for being unable to provide for themselves and their children.

Israel was the laughingstock for her neighbours. They ridiculed her and spewed insults upon her. Oh, the pains were overbearing! At times they felt helpless, even to the point of death. However, the lady (Israel) became no longer the subject of ridicule but the object of prosperity. God Almighty, her Lover and Life came to the rescue.

Israel was delivered from a dearth that threatened the very core of her existence. God said to the dearth, "Your time has expired. No more crumbs for My wife. Israel shall eat of lush green pastures and will rest in peace beside still waters." God put to an end all that famine which caused disaster upon the land.

Have you ever been in a famine? Are you facing a famine now that seems unending? Dearth has affected your person, health, money, emotional state, and everything else. Oh yes, friend, your famine may be physical, spiritual, mental, emotional, or even financial. It may seem as though whatever you put your hands to is going nowhere. It would appear that there is no success. The famine has starved you of everything.

Today, I speak to you that your famine is over. The dearth that has engulfed you has been for far too long. But God is telling you, "No more." Yes beloved, the lack and scarcity is over. It is time that you accept what God is giving you. He is not partial and if He makes one rich, why then will He not do the same for you? You belong to Him and He cares for you, so just believe Him, and do whatever He asks you to do.

It is time for the uncleanness to go, and those ridiculing you will be no more. Your days of plenty are here. Those days of disgrace are gone. Almighty God is doing a new thing. The days of lack are gone into oblivion, ensuring no more crumbs. Believe Him and act on His commands. It is the time of increase. *Shalom.*

Day 53

"This is what The Sovereign Lord says: On the day I cleanse you from all your sins, I will resettle your towns, and the ruins will be rebuilt. The desolate land will be cultivated instead of lying desolate in the sight of all who pass through it."

Eze 36:33-34

Once Waste, Now Fertile

The land of Israel was laid bare. It was desolate and barren because of the sins of its citizens. The soil refused to produce crops to sustain the Israelites, and they faced untold hardship. It was God's intention to make the land of Israel fertile once more. However, before fertility took place, cleansing had to be applied to the people.

You see, beloved, the contamination of the land was a result of the sins committed by its inhabitants. Ah, friends, the very physical Earth responded to the wickedness of those who corrupted it. Beloved, the very elements which produced life in man, when disrespected and mocked will become affected. Man was created from the Earth and it was The Breath of Almighty God that gave him life. Therefore, when man sins, both the material from which he came, and the Giver of Life are seriously affected.

Oh, friends, did you know that our environment reacts to the way we live and behave? Let us then be careful to live right, being mindful of how we interact with God, the Earth, the environment, humans, and ourselves. Almighty God will operate in accordance with how we interact with the various elements around us. A simple lesson is, whenever we damage the environment, we, and those after us will suffer the consequences of our foolish actions.

God, therefore, had to step in to save the land of Israel after it was contaminated. He first cleansed the residents of the land. Then, He fertilized the land and once more the land that was desolate and barren became fruitful. Oh, what a God! Did you know that He takes note of everything and makes record? Oh, brothers and sisters, He is The Great and Mighty Recorder!

Today, there is so much bloodshed, sexual sin, idolatry, unyielded hearts and more that have contaminated the land of Jamaica. The very Earth we occupy is crying out because of the abomination caused to it. Unrepentant sins have caused desolation to the Earth and separation from God. God is unhappy about the evil in the nation. God, however, has been entreating people of the land to repent and turn to Him. The repentance includes all who are separated from Him. No one is exempt, from leaders to peasants.

Maybe it is not clear to many that the Prime Minister and Government Ministers hold the key to stop much of what is happening in our nation today. If our Prime Minister comes publicly and truly repents of his sins, and turns to Almighty God, God will hear and start the deliverance process in this nation. Murders will be reduced considerably, and people will start living right. If the leadership of a country knows Jesus Christ as Lord and Saviour, that nation will prosper. On the other hand, if the leadership is corrupt and has no time for God, many of the citizens will adopt that kind of lifestyle. Jamaica as a nation is suffering. When will we wake up?

Yes, beloved, yesterday's devotional informed that the dearth has expired and there are no more crumbs. To solidify that point, the land has moved from waste to fertility. Since the land is now fertile, may we make good use of it. God has called us to operate the land since it is fertile. Both in the natural and the spiritual, the land is rich. Make use of it. The harvest is ripe, but the labourers are few. Yes, beloved, it is time to harvest the souls of many who continue to languish in sin.

In the land of Jamaica, although wickedness is at an all-time high, it is ripe for evangelism. Let us go out and preach the Gospel of Jesus Christ to a lost people. Ripe and fertile is the land for evangelism. May we as Christians do our part and win souls for Heaven.

Day 54

"They will say, This land that was laid waste has become like the Garden of Eden; the cities that were lying in ruins, desolate and destroyed, are now fortified and inhabited."

Eze 36:35

Beauty for Ashes on Full Display

When the Sovereign Lord makes someone beautiful, elegance and delight will be noticed from near and far by others. Sin is absolutely ugly. Whenever one lives in it, that individual has absorbed the ugliness of the master of sin, Satan himself. On the outside, one may look pretty, but if sin is one's master, then ugliness permeates from the inside. True beauty evolves from within. Satan's ways and deeds are just pure evil, and evil is virtually ugly. The Devil himself may sport a handsome look on the outside but he is ugly.

The land of Israel was not only desolate, but disgrace polluted the very core of Israel because of the people's sin. God, however, changed all of that and replaced the ugliness of sin with the beauty of His holiness. It became like the Garden of Eden that lacked nothing good. The beauty was on display.

When God's holiness is upon anyone, such an individual has been transformed from a life of sin. However, there are days of suffering and pain, difficulty and hardship which cause ashes to spew upon the lives of many of God's children. Hardship has a way of disfiguring many good people and years of sufferings can cause ugliness.

To you beloved who are suffering, God is giving you beauty for ashes. Your years of crying and uncomfortable experiences have fast come to an end. The favour of God has now located you. Your years of misery are over. The Lord your God is giving you beauty for ashes. In Isaiah 61:2b-3, the prophet echoed loudly for you in the following,

> "To comfort all who mourn and provide for those who grieve in Zion. To bestow on them a crown of beauty instead of ashes, the oil of gladness instead of mourning, and a garment of praise instead of a spirit of despair. They will be called oaks of righteousness, a planting of The Lord for the display of His splendour."

Oh yes, beloved, in the sight of man, you did not look so good, and things were dull for you. On the outside, you showcased hurt and pain. But now, all of that is changing. God is giving you beauty for ashes.

A garment of praise you are now robed in instead of that old cloak of despair. Yes, beloved, your old ashes are blown away by God's spiritual wind. Thus, you are radiating the beauty of Jesus Christ and people cannot avoid seeing the magnificence ensued. Albert Orsborn captured the believer's state of beauty and penned,

> Let the beauty of Jesus be seen in me
> All His wonderful passion and purity
> O Thou Spirit Divine, all my nature refine
> Till the beauty of Jesus be seen in me.

Yes, beloved, when ashes are replaced by beauty, the inner man is first transformed. Remember, God first purified the Israelites before allowing them to inhabit the new land. So now with a transformed nature, believers, we reflect the beauty of Jesus.

Once, a load of cares disfigured your outward appearance and the hardship was easily recognized on your face. Now your nature is transformed by God's glorious presence making you beautiful. Your beauty has radiated from the inside out. Your beauty is showing brilliantly. Those who knew you before as down and depressed are seeing the joy of the Lord on show. Yes, beloved, God has given you beauty for ashes.

Day 55

"They shall say, this land that was desolate is become like the Garden of Eden; and the waste and desolate and ruined cities are become fenced, and are inhabited. Then the heathen that are left round about you shall know that I plant that, that was desolate: I The Lord have spoken it, and I will do it."

Eze 36:35-36

They Shall Know When the Lord Has Done the Work

"This is the Lord's doing, and wonderful are His deeds!" Such an expression is often uttered when Almighty God does something exceptional, like bringing someone back from the dead. He is still raising the dead.

Israel was practically dead and about to be buried by her neighbours. But the Sovereign Lord pulled off a great feat. He rescued Israel, cleansed her, gave her beauty for ashes, and then set her on a pedestal adorned in magnificent beauty. Her enemies who had planned to bury her now saw her as the talk of the world. They exclaimed not for her once ravaged lifestyle but for her exceeding beauty. Only Almighty God had the power to resurrect a dying Israel. Then, He made her the envy of her neighbours.

Israel's neighbours were numerous and filled with great hatred towards her, yet they could not touch her. All they could do was respond to the truth: the now transformed Israel was a work done by her God. Even the enemy could recognize when God blessed Israel and made her beautiful.

Your blessings are from God. Whenever it is time to be lavished by Him, your former lifestyle will be a thing of the past. There shall be a generated beauty. The beauty generated shall be seen by many, including your enemies who hated you from near and far. What a God!

The shocking truth is, when God blesses an individual, a family, or even a nation, the blessing received can be of an enormous proportion and will be evident to many. When it was difficult, it was rough, tough, and hard. So, when God blesses, He may bless you proportionately according to the equivalence of your troubles and heartaches. He gives you double for your troubles and take you from nothingness to great possession. Just as the Garden of Eden was clothed in consummate beauty and on display to the world, so it is with you. God's blessings upon you are evident to all. The doing is not by man but by Almighty God.

Dearly beloved, God has adorned you with great blessings. Your enemies are seeing what He is doing, and they can only exclaim, "Look what God has done!"

Day 56

"Then the nations around you that remain will know that I The Lord have rebuilt what was destroyed and have replanted what was desolate. I The Lord have spoken, and I will do it."

Eze 36:36

Who Can Stop Him?

Can Almighty God be stopped? Is mortal man capable of stopping the Sovereign One? Ah, beloved, can Satan and his demons limit or stop the One True God? Oh, no! No one can and no one will. Almighty God cannot be stopped. He is Undefeated, Undisputed, Omnipotent, Omnipresent, Omniscient, Immutable, Perfect, and Incomparable. What an awesome God is He! The Mighty Unstoppable One.

It was God's time of intimacy with His wife Israel. She was no longer estranged from Him. God was ready to rebuild and bless her with elegance and stunning poise. He was ready to make her land once more flow with milk and honey. His blessing for her was unprecedented and no one was going to stop Him from doing what He wanted to do. The devil and his demons were powerless to stop Him. Israel's neighbours were incapable of stopping Him, looking on in fear and amazement.

Dearly beloved, when the Sovereign Lord is ready to bless you, no one can stop Him. No one can. I say no one. No obeah man or woman can stop Him, as they are all pitiful. Your supervisor, principal, or manager who has done everything to stop your promotion cannot stop this one. Your boss or supervisor is unable to hold you down any longer. Their intention against you was purely motivated by a spirit of jealousy, control, and wickedness. Yet not even that evil demon can stop God from elevating you. It is God's timing with you.

Who can stop the Lord? No one can and no one will. Todd Dulaney's (2016) song entitled, 'Victory Belongs to Jesus' is a fitting tribute to The Unstoppable One. Let us sing along.

> Who will stand against the Lord?
> No one can,
> No one will.
>
> Who will stand against the King?
> No one can,
> No one will.
>
> Oh oh oh
> Oh oh oh
> Victory belongs to Jesus
> Victory belongs to Him
>
> Oh oh oh
> Oh oh oh
> Victory belongs to Jesus
> Victory belongs to Him
>
> We put our trust in You
> Yes, we put our hope in You.
> You will deliver,
> You're a Provider
> I find my victory in You
>
> Forever victorious,
> Forever we win
> I find my victory in You.

I said, who can stand (who can stand against the Lord?)
No one can (no one can)
No one (no one will)

Yes, who can stand (who can stand against the King?)
Nobody can (no one can)
No one will (no one will)

Yeah yeah

Oh, oh oh
Oh, oh oh

Say the victory belongs to Jesus (victory belongs to Jesus)
(Yes, it does!) Victory belongs to Him

Oh, oh oh
Oh, oh oh!

Victory.

Yes beloved, the Victorious Almighty God, Creator of the Universe, is our Elevator. No one can stop Him from lifting us up. No one can, no one will.

Day 57

"Thus saith The Lord God; I will yet for this be inquired of by the House of Israel, to do it for them; I will increase them with men like a flock."

Eze 36:37

The Increase: A Promise to be Fulfilled

When the Israelites served idols, their requests to God were denied by Him. Formerly, Almighty God did not listen to them. He refused to be inquired of by them as their hearts were far away from Him. However, since God renewed the relationship between Himself and them by giving them a new heart, He was not only ready to hear them but was keen to listen to their inquiries.

Since the communication passage between God and Israel had no more barriers, the Israelites were commissioned to pray to Almighty God for His blessings to come upon them. The increase was a must, but they were supposed to ask God for the increase. Inquiring of God by Israel through prayer suggests that Israel was now dependent on God to sustain them.

Inquiring of God is all about glorifying Him. The Israelites' hearts were once far from God. They were hitched to lifeless idols, an abomination to the Lord. However, with their hearts being new, they clung to Almighty God and sought Him with their new heart, thus glorifying Him. Friends, only a new heart can glorify God. In 2 Corinthians 5:17 the Apostle Paul revealed, "Therefore if any man be in Christ, he is a new creature: old things are passed away; behold, all things are become new." Ah, beloved, Israel received a new heart. They demonstrated a new lifestyle, and they had the right to consult God.

Israel became a nation of promise and possibility. They belonged to the One True God. Being a people of promise, they needed to inquire of God for the promises made to them. Their eyes were centred upon Him, with their desires to be filled.

The promise was for Israel to become as numerous as flocks. Concerning Almighty God, flocks were designed for His holy purpose. They were to be used for sacrifice presented to Him. Thus, the people mightily increased, and they were a quality sacrifice unto the Lord. Oh, yes — with new hearts, they were presented to Jehovah as a living sacrifice in a brand-new land.

In Romans 12:1-2, Paul purported,

> "I beseech you therefore, brethren, by the mercies of God, that ye present your bodies a living sacrifice, holy, acceptable unto God, which is your reasonable service. Be not conformed to this world: but be ye transformed by the renewing of your mind, that ye may prove what is that good, and acceptable, and perfect will of God."

True sacrifice to God begins with the heart which is the spirit of man. That sacrificed spirit is renewed in the image of God. Israel was renewed, thus their inquiries to Almighty God for His promise of grace, mercy, provision, and other blessings could never be denied. What a position to be in! What a nation (Israel) being benefactors! What a God, Great Jehovah, who listens and answers the inquiring of the hearts of His dear children of Israel!

Dearly beloved, we who are Christians have been imputed with new hearts. We qualify as legitimate children of the Most High God. Being children of God, allow us to inquire of Him. Yes, beloved, the avenue is created by the Blessed Holy Spirit. He lives in us and joins us to Jesus Christ, our wonderful Lord. We can now say without a doubt, "Abba," my Father, my Friend, and my God.

We have received a real privilege to inquire of the Only True God. His mercies are new every morning and great is His faithfulness. Therefore, let us inquire of Him for His mercies, both for ourselves and others. Our position is unique! Our position is safe! Our position is real! Our hearts are new and upon this basis, our inquiring of God will never be denied. Almighty God has promised us that He will answer when we inquire. Oh yes, brothers and sisters, God promises us that He will come through. Consequently, an increase is inevitable.

Friend, you are qualified for your increase. Inquire of your Heavenly Father. So, go ahead and ask, as it will be given! Seek and you shall find! Knock because the door will be opened unto you! Certainly, you will not be denied.

Day 58

"As the holy flock, as the flock of Jerusalem in her solemn feasts; so shall the waste cities be filled with flocks of men: and they shall know that I Am The Lord."

Eze 36:38

Chosen

Almighty God had filled the former empty cities with people, His flock. A striking comparison is realized with the vast flocks of sacrificial animals normally carried to Jerusalem at the three great annual feasts, known as Passover, Pentecost, and Feast of Tabernacles. As those animals were devoted to God for sacrificial purpose, the people of Israel were also dedicated to the Lord for sacrifice.

Animals were chosen by God to be dedicated to Him for sacrifice. Just as it was with the animals going up to Jerusalem, so it was for the people chosen by God. They were dedicated to His service, to be offered up to the Lord.

It is clear then, that as children of God, we were chosen by God long before He laid the foundation of the Earth. Yes, we are His choice possession. However, our formalisation took place when we accepted Jesus Christ as Lord and Saviour. We were washed in His blood, saved, sanctified, and filled with His Holy Spirit. Our dedication to the service to Almighty God now sanctions us as living sacrifices unto the Lord. Our lives, therefore, are His. We should offer up true worship to Him.

Day 59

"The Hand of The Lord was upon me, and He brought me out by The Spirit of The Lord and set me in the middle of a valley; it was full of bones. He led me to and fro among them, and I saw a great many bones on the floor of the valley, bones that were very dry. He asked me, "Son of man, can these bones live?" I said, "O Sovereign Lord, You alone know."

Eze 37:1-3

Can These Bones Live?

In previous chapters of Ezekiel, both Israel and Judah were threatened with inevitable destruction by Almighty God. They were so threatened because of their sins against the One True God. Idolatry was the chief sin that both Israel and Judah perpetrated against God. They insulted Almighty God by prostrating themselves to idols. As a result, God drove them out of their land into exile. Many of them were expelled many miles beyond their borders. They who were God's people, and the apple of His eyes became His enemies. They were passionate about their lifestyle of idolatry that they gave all they had into it.

Through visions to Ezekiel, God promised restoration and deliverance to them because death was everywhere. Israel and Judah were desperate, destitute, demised, distressed, doomed, dry, destroyed, and so down that Almighty God compared them to dry bones. They were dead and needed to be resurrected.

"Can these dry bones live?" Is resurrection possible? Let us explore in the coming days devotionals.

Day 60

"The Hand of The Lord was upon me, and He brought me out by The Spirit of The Lord and set me in the middle of a valley; it was full of bones. He led me to and fro among them, and I saw a great many bones on the floor of the valley, bones that were very dry. He asked me, "Son of man, can these bones live?" I said, "O Sovereign Lord, You alone know."

Eze 37:1-3

The Dead Church!

Today, some churches cannot grow because they are dead. Anything dead cannot grow since there is nothing or no one with life sustaining it. It is a pity that many who are known to be Christians are experiencing deadness. However, how can anyone be in Christ Jesus, yet experiences deadness?

Ah, beloved, it is a sin when the Holy Spirit is not in full control of the life of an individual or church. It is so sad today that certain individuals are in control of their church as Almighty God is placed at the back of the church. He is not consulted or just barely sought after. Some say the church belongs to God, but their actions speak differently. Others say, this is my church and I run it. Everything concerning their Church must come through them. However, the Holy Spirit must be in complete control of the church. If He is, there is absolutely no deadness as growth is inevitable.

Many are already dead and living outside the will of God. They may think they are alive, but anyone or anything outside God's will is dead. Ezekiel was placed in a position where there were dead all around. He was asked the awkward question, "Can these dry bones live?" The House of Israel was dead and scattered amongst the nations, but something supernatural was about to take place. The resurrection power of Almighty God was about to pay a special visit to the dry bones. Permission for resurrection was granted. God sanctioned the move to bring the nation of Israel back to life. Resurrection was possible.

Beloved, not everything needs to be resurrected. Some things are better off dead. Some past relationships need to remain dead for fresh life to sprout elsewhere. Consequently, do not try to resurrect what God has not sanctioned. However, if you are put in the position by God to raise the dead, then you have work to be done.

While standing in the valley of dry bones, Ezekiel could have said, "It's best to move from the valley of the dead as there are too many dead bones here. Only dead desires and dead plans are around that have caused deadness to spread." Ezekiel could also have said, "If I stay amongst the dead, it is likely that I will be numbered amongst them." However, he did not resort to that attitude because resurrection was possible.

Ezekiel's position amongst the dead was for a purpose that would transform the trajectory of Israel's landscape forever. Therefore, as God asked him, "Can these dry bones live?" "Thou Lord, You knowest," was the response.

It is possible that God will send you to a place where there is death all around, but He does not expect you to be dead. What He expects of you is to resurrect the dead. If you stay amongst the dead doing nothing, it is likely that you will end up dead. Therefore, do not just look at the volume of the dead. Do not do anything else apart from what God tells you.

Ah, beloved, the spiritually dead cannot worship God. It does not matter how well you prompt, beat upon or entreat, a dead person will still not worship God. You could be in a congregation and keep begging people to praise God, but if persons are dead, they cannot praise God. Understand this, the dead is dead.

Ezekiel saw the dry bones, but to use a whip to beat the bones to live once more made no sense. In the same way, there is no application one can prescribe that will work upon the dead to offer spiritual life except resurrection. Only with this is resurrection possible.

Day 61

Then He said to me, "Prophesy to these bones and say to them, dry bones, hear the word of The Lord! This is what The Sovereign Lord says to these bones: I will make breath enter you, and you will come to life. I will attach tendons to you and make flesh come upon you and cover you with skin; I will put breath in you, and you will come to life. Then you will know that I Am The Lord."

Eze 37:4-6

There is Life in the Word

God asked Ezekiel an audacious question. "Can these dry bones live?" He then gave Ezekiel a command to prophesy to the dead dry bones. The prophetic word of God spoken in dead situations can produce life, since the dead can hear the prophetic word. The Jewish people, though dead and scattered amongst the nations, were never forgotten. God remembered their deadened state and planned to restore them to life. Clearly, no created power had the ability to restore dried out human bones to life. Only God had such authority to cause restoration to dry out bones. Yes indeed, beloved, He used Ezekiel to speak over the bones. Through the prophetic word spoken, resurrection was possible since the dead bones had the ability to hear the prophetic words from Ezekiel's lips. Ah, beloved! This is awesomeness.

In Genesis 1, a vivid picture of Almighty God is painted using words to produce life. He spoke the world into existence when He said, "Let there be …." and subsequently, whatever He summoned, appeared. So powerful were those words that they produced life. God knew what He wanted, and surely Israel would once more become a nation that would offer up praises and true worship to Him. Those dried out bones would once more have skin and flesh all over them. Also, the wind would be prophesied to, giving life.

Fellow Christians, there are many dry bones around us, and Almighty God has called us to prophesy life to them. Those who have not accepted Jesus Christ as Lord and Saviour are dried out by sin. In their unrepentant state they are dead in sin and trespasses. Their dead state is sorrowful and, although some of them will not admit to it, we need to prophesy life to them.

The word that God has placed in us has the power to resurrect the dead. It was Ezekiel's relationship with his God that caused Almighty God to trust him with the task of speaking to dead bones. Likewise, we are also trusted with the undiluted word of God to speak to those dead in sin. The words spoken to the dead have the power to resurrect them. Do not just sit idly by with the word of God, saying they will not listen. Our duty is to speak life into the dead, so let us prophesy the word of God.

Therefore, brothers and sisters, may we keep in mind that the same God who told Ezekiel to prophesy to dead bones is asking us to speak His word to hearts of people who are deadened by sin. Remember, there's life in the word, and consequently, resurrection is possible.

Day 62

"I will lay sinews upon you, and will bring up flesh upon you, and cover you with skin, and put breath in you, and ye shall live; and ye shall know that I Am The Lord."

Eze 37:6

The Breath of Almighty God

Almighty God told Ezekiel what to do and what He Himself would do. They were both to work together to have the once dead nation of Israel returned to life. That would happen through resurrection.

The key element that gives life is the Breath of God. Consequently, God revealed that He would put breath into that which was once dead, to bring about life. The nation of Israel was about to receive life once again, and resurrection was possible.

In Genesis 1:26a, God said, "Let us make man in our own image, after our likeness." It was obvious that God was speaking to at least Another Person. But to whom? At this juncture, the introduction of the Trinity is evident, and it happened for the creation of man. How special man is to God! Israel was indeed special to Him and God was about to resurrect a dead nation.

For emphasis, whilst the word Trinity, Triunity and Triune are not mentioned in the Bible, references to these concepts are recorded. The word Trinity is derived from the Latin word *trinitas,* which has to do with three-fold. Triune, Triunity or Trinity has to do with a group consisting of three closely related members united as One. In Genesis 1:26a, this mention is made. The union of three divine persons, the Father, the Son, and the Holy Spirit, is seen in One Divine God. These three in one possess the same substance, being coequal, coexistent, consubstantial, and coeternal is described as *Elohim*. *Elohim* is one of God's names and therefore, suggest that God is all powerful and infinite and only He has the power to resurrect.

Therefore, watch God work in Genesis 2:7, "Then The Lord God formed a man from the dust of the ground and breathed into his nostrils The Breath of Life, and the man became a living being." God breathed the Breath of Life into a dead body lying on the ground and subsequently, man became alive. This is clear that the very Breath of Almighty God produced life. Therefore, with an entire nation, dead, the same God who breathed the Breath of Life into a dead body and life appeared, was about to perform a major operation to bring back Israel, thus, resurrection was possible.

The Breath of Life was breathed into a body lying on the ground and Adam became alive. The same Sovereign God decided to put breath into the bones covered in flesh and skin. The nation of Israel at that moment was about to experience the resurrection power of God.

Today, the same God is ready to breathe life into some who are dead in their sins. As Israel was dead and about to be buried, so it is with those dead in sin. Satan is waiting to bury them in Hell. However, the Breath of God, the Blessed Holy Spirit is here, ready to breathe into the spiritually dead to produce spiritual life. Resurrection is possible.

About the Author

Geoffrey Gordon graduated from the College of Theological and Interdisciplinary Studies (CTIS), Jamaica Theological Seminary (JTS) and the Caribbean Graduate School of Theology (CGST) with honours. He is a Probation Officer and has been a Christian for more than 30 years. He is a member of the Giblatore Baptist Church in St. Catherine, Jamaica. He also lectures theology at the College of Theological and Interdisciplinary Studies and at the Eglington School of Theology. He is a Preacher and Bible teacher. He is married and lives in the parish of Manchester.